Early Music: A Very Short Introduction

Very Short Introductions available now:

Available soon:

For more information visit our web site
www.oup.co.uk/general/vsi/

Thomas Forrest Kelly

EARLY MUSIC

A Very Short Introduction

OXFORD
UNIVERSITY PRESS

Oxford University Press, Inc., publishes works that further
Oxford University's objective of excellence
in research, scholarship, and education.

Oxford   New York
Auckland   Cape Town   Dar es Salaam   Hong Kong   Karachi
Kuala Lumpur   Madrid   Melbourne   Mexico City   Nairobi
New Delhi   Shanghai   Taipei   Toronto

With offices in
Argentina   Austria   Brazil   Chile   Czech Republic   France   Greece
Guatemala   Hungary   Italy   Japan   Poland   Portugal   Singapore
South Korea   Switzerland   Thailand   Turkey   Ukraine   Vietnam

Copyright © 2011 by Thomas Forrest Kelly

Published by Oxford University Press, Inc.
198 Madison Avenue, New York, NY 10016

www.oup.com

Oxford is a registered trademark of Oxford University Press

Library of Congress Cataloging-in-Publication Data
Kelly, Thomas Forrest.
Early music: a very short introduction / Thomas Forrest Kelly.
p. cm.—(Very short introductions)
Includes bibliographical references and index.
ISBN 978-0-19-973076-6 (pbk.)
1. Performance practice (Music).
2. Music—Interpretation (Phrasing, dynamics, etc.).
3. Music—500–1400—History and criticism.
4. Music—15th century—History and criticism.
5. Music—16th century—History and criticism.
6. Music—17th century—History and criticism.   I. Title.
ML457.K45 2011
780.9—dc22
2010039421

1 3 5 7 9 8 6 4 2

Printed in Great Britain
by Ashford Colour Press Ltd., Gosport, Hants.
on acid-free paper

To Peggy

Acknowledgments

With thanks I acknowledge the assistance of the following friends and colleagues, who generously read drafts of this text, and made helpful suggestions: Peggy Badenhausen, Lisa Goode Crawford, Ross Duffin, Benjamin Dunham, Stephen Hammer, Paul Hillier, Dennis Olsen, Stephen Stubbs.

Contents

List of illustrations

Chapter 1

What does "early music" mean?

This is a book about the music of the past. Medieval, Renaissance, and Baroque music have been repeatedly discarded and rediscovered ever since they were new. For me and for many readers, the music is beautiful and intriguing; it expands our horizons and nourishes our souls.

An interest in music of the past has been characteristic of a part of the musical world since the early nineteenth century—from about the time of the rise of museums. The revival of Gregorian chant in the early nineteenth century, the "Cecilian movement" in later nineteenth-century Germany seeking to immortalize Palestrina's music as a sound ideal, Mendelssohn's revival of Bach—these are some of the efforts made in the past to restore still earlier music.

In recent years this interest has taken on particular meaning, representing two specific trends: first, a rediscovery of little-known and under-appreciated repertories, and second, an effort to recover lost performing styles, in the conviction that such music will come to life anew using those performance practices. Medieval, Renaissance, and Baroque music have been central to these ideas, and their repertories have taken on new sheen and attractiveness as a result.

Much was gained in the twentieth century from the study and revival of instruments, playing techniques, and repertories. What began as a "movement" akin to the arts-and-crafts movement took on political overtones in the 1960s, fueled by a sense of return to the natural, a rebellion against received wisdom and enforced conformity, and a notion that early music was a participant's music as much as it was a listener's. The enormous success of a few performers and groups has more recently tended to professionalize early music, and the amateur, participatory aspect has faded somewhat.

Why revive old music?

There is already so much music in the world, so much being created every day, so much readily available in broadcast and recording media, that we can never listen to all of it. Why then do we make such an effort to revive music of the past? A variety of reasons suggest themselves: exoticism; history; novelty; politics; and, finally, pleasure.

Early music is like "world music" in the sense that it provides listeners with something outside their own culture, their own tradition, their own experience. This is in essence the appeal of forgotten repertories; those not yet forgotten may be canonical, they may be highbrow, they may be elitist, but they are not exotic. These earlier repertories provide a means of connecting with worlds so different from our own that they give us reason to question our assumptions about how music works, what it does, and what it should sound like.

There is also the desire to know what it was that people in the past listened to. What are those angels singing and playing in medieval paintings? What are those musicians up in the balcony in that banquet-scene doing? What did Queen Elizabeth I dance to? What entertained Louis XIV at dinner? These are questions more historical than musical, in that we're not at first seeking musical pleasure but historical knowledge, in an attempt to make a well-rounded historical picture of a time and place distant from us but of considerable interest. If it turns out that we like the music, so much the better; no one would question admiring a Gothic cathedral or a painting by Van Eyck or Leonardo. Lovers of the visual arts are almost never forced to justify their love of those things, but the music of the past often does not get the same timeless respect. The impetus for this aspect of early music is essentially historical, like the interest in medieval cookery, or in Baroque clothing.

Sheer novelty can also be at the core of an interest in early music. It is not like any music today; and it is not like any music in other cultures; and it is not even like itself, in that it consists of a long and broad series of repertories that have in common only that they are old and unknown. There is a certain satisfaction, perhaps, in being the first person in a long time to hear a Spinacino intabulation for lute of a sixteenth-century frottola; and satisfaction in showing off—that is, introducing other listeners to it.

The protest movements of the 1960s and 1970s—civil rights, antiwar, and the like—produced what many called a "counterculture" resisting all that was passed down as traditional and elitist. To the extent that early music was seen as nontraditional, and participatory (there were, and are, a great many summer workshops where early music is played), it could be seen as part of a cultural trend toward music of the people, music without pretense, music that expresses a general union of popular and learned. It cannot be sheer coincidence that the early-music "movement," as it is sometimes called, arose at the same time as a number of other popular and popularist movements: the folk-music revival, for example, propelled by Pete Seeger, Alan Lomax, and others.

Tradition and interruption

Almost all music in the world of concert, or art, or classical music, is (a) heard electronically, and (b) old. Many more people listen to music on recordings or broadcasts than actually hear it live. And many more people prefer music they already know to music they have not yet heard; even music of contemporary composers is seldom heard live, or at first performances. One of the attractions of jazz, and of live concerts of rock and other music, is a sense of being there, of being present at a unique event that nobody else has ever heard. There is an excitement in the improvisatory, real-time experience that is generally lacking in concert music, whose artists read from printed music and reproduce a piece we've heard before, and likewise lacking when we listen to a recording, even of a jazz or other improvisation. There's no risk in a recording.

A substantial part of the activity of the modern early-music movement is an effort to evoke that excitement, the one-time, you-were-there effect of music being made *now*. Part of the recapturing is done by reviving music that has not been heard before—at least by us, now—and part of it is by recapturing the performing styles—including improvisation, ornamentation, and other expressive effect—that have been lost in the modern performers' training to be an exact reproducer of the notes on the page. How successfully the early-music revival reaches these aims is subject to ongoing debate, but the impetus for its existence is grounded in the idea of spontaneity, of excitement, and of recapturing experiences otherwise lost to us.

Until the late nineteenth century, if you wanted to hear music you had to know how to perform it, or you had to be physically present in the place and at the time that it was performed. The *performance* of music had a value that it perhaps has lost, even though music itself—defined differently by every listener—has enormous value to almost everybody.

Now, with recording and playback devices we can hear any music, from any place, from any repertory in history, and at any moment we wish. We can have an enormous orchestra in our living room, and we can command it to stop while we step out to the kitchen for a moment—and then command the Mahler symphony to continue. It is quite remarkable.

And with a century of recordings behind us we have a backlog of recorded performances that grant us amazing access to performance events that took place in the past, and to a wide variety of repertories and styles. We can also tell, by listening to performance styles change over time, that there is no *one way* that any particular piece gets performed, at least not over the last century's recorded documentation.

There may still be those who claim that they play a particular piece of music the way Bach did, because they play it the way their teacher does, who studied with so-and-so in Vienna, who studied with so-and-so, who studied with Czerny, who studied with Beethoven, and so on back to Bach; these players have probably not listened to the changes that the piece in question has undergone in a century of recorded music; if they had, they would probably come to doubt the fixity of tradition and the unity of performing style.

Even if we believed in unbroken and unwavering tradition, early-music advocates would argue that there are certain performance traditions that are broken beyond recovery. During the French Revolution, for example, legend has it that harpsichords from the ancien régime were burned for firewood. When real professional music teaching was begun in the Paris Conservatoire after the revolution, there was an unbridgeable gap between what had gone before in the eighteenth century—essentially late Baroque music and before—and what was now being taught at the Conservatoire. Even if we believed in the stern tradition of method, passed down from teacher to pupil, we could not trace it much farther back than the early part of the nineteenth century.

And so the music from before that time, usually taught and performed, only as exercises—Bach preludes and fugues for pianists, his trio sonatas for organists, Italian Baroque arias as exercises and recital-openers for singers, all performed in "modern," nineteenth-century style—was thought to be lost to us, both as a regularly performed repertory and as a style that we know how to perform.

The early-music movement seeks to reexamine that music; its repertory is the music before the common-practice, canonical music of the concert hall, the modern chamber music concert, the current opera house; it seeks to understand the context in which that older music, that now seems so odd, was not only perfectly normal but thought to be ravishingly beautiful.

Early music has another aspect that has to do with performance: how the music is performed, not what the music is. This emphasis on performance is one of the two main aspects of the movement— the notion that lost practices and broken traditions can be recovered through assiduous research and practice.

The hardworking pioneers of the 1960s and 1970s sought to find out, by the study and reproduction of instruments of the past, what could be learned about sound and about what works best when Bach is played on a harpsichord rather than a Steinway, when Corelli is played on a gut-strung, lower-pitched, lighter-bowed violin; and some performers made an effort to rediscover playing techniques and stylistic conventions from the careful study of surviving writings about music, and from a careful reexamination of surviving scores. Works such as Carl Philip Emanuel Bach's *Essay on the True Art of Keyboard-Playing* (1753), Johann Joachim Quantz's *Instructions for Playing the Transverse Flute* (1752), and Leopold Mozart's *Essay on a Complete Violin-Method* (1756) became sources of information about performance of late-Baroque music. The effort to take the authors at their word and to ferret out of these books information useful to modern performers was a work of real intensity, carried out by those who believed it could be done.

Believing it could be done depends of course on what "it" is. There is no doubt that a great deal was learned by those pioneering scholarly and performing efforts, and anybody who has been listening to Baroque music since the 1960s will know how much has changed since those efforts began.

What "it" is can perhaps be approached by what "it" is not: it is not a single, unified, unchallengeable method of performance, by the use of which any piece of music can be played in an "authentic" fashion; that would be a formula completely at odds with what most eighteenth-century writers say about good taste, about expression, about feeling, and about playing differently in different circumstances—all of which make clear that no two performances are alike. And it is not focused on the music of a single place and time, unlike these treatises, all of which come from mid-eighteenth-century German-speaking lands—which, interesting as it is, is neither central to music-making nor the only place and time of interest to people who make music. (There were other early writers on music—including John Dowland and François Couperin—but nothing quite as encyclopedic as these writers in German.)

The focus on these treatises was an important start, and all who were involved in those efforts felt proud of what was learned, and of the vigor and freshness that Baroque music seemed to gain. It was an important part of the spirit of the time to feel that one was a pioneer, that one was rediscovering, through hard work, a tradition that had been lost. Now, a generation or more later, there are teachers who learned from these pioneers, and students can simply go to a conservatory or to a summer workshop and learn the modern approach to Baroque music at the hands of people who have been practicing this style their whole lives, second-generation practitioners who never had to unlearn the Romantic approach to Bach and Handel. Perhaps some of the excitement of the discovery has been lost, but it is certainly true that standards have improved considerably.

These pioneers were involved in an attempt to find a contemporaneous performance style for the music, on the assumption—and it is an assumption that not everyone will grant—that composers and listeners and performers at any given place and time were a nexus of understanding, and that the music speaks best when it speaks its own language. Some will object that it is well and good for those people, but that we are not those people, we are ourselves and we are now, and we cannot un-listen to the music we have all around us, and so performers might just as well acknowledge the existence of pianos, microphones, amplifiers, modern keyboard techniques using thumbs, the need for loud instruments and voice to fill large halls, and so on. To those people many early-music enthusiasts will probably shrug and wish them well; but even the users of modern hardware could adapt some aspects of historical style that might affect their performances—a suitable tempo, for example, can transform a piece regardless of the instrument it is played on.

But early music has another side, and that is the music itself—that is, not only the rediscovery of lost traditions, but the rediscovery of lost music; repertories that for one reason or another have fallen out of use, or out of favor, and that when rediscovered and revived might give considerable musical pleasure.

Lost repertories

Music is "lost" when nobody can remember it. If somebody figures out a way to write it down, and that writing can serve as a recipe for performing the music again, then of course it is not lost. The musical notation developed in medieval Europe has made it possible to know about a great deal of music that nobody remembers personally. The amount of detail encoded in the musical notation varies with time and with writing system and with writer, but the level of detail generally increases with time, and wherever we have music that is written down, or wherever we have living musicians, we have the possibility of music.

Most of our concert music is performed by a combination of notation and remembering; few people give concerts where they are sight-reading. Either they have memorized the music—usually using notation—like performers at most piano or vocal recitals, or they read from music but have practiced many times before performing—like most orchestral concerts. Where only memory is available, there is the risk of forgetting, or of slippage of memory from one performance to the next. And where only notation is used, there is the risk that the player will not fully understand the notation, or that the notation, as is almost always true, will be specific about some things (usually the pitches and lengths of the notes) but not about others (often dynamics, articulation, volume, tone color). It leaves out what is taken for granted and must be supplied by the performer; this is a lot of what is worked out in rehearsal.

Early music concerns itself mostly with music where some notation survives, but nobody remembers the music. To perform the music, one needs to understand as much as possible about what the notation means; and to understand what is *not* present in the notation, or suggested but not specified, and be sure to include those essentials also.

Questions that have concerned musicians seeking to understand older repertories are sometimes quite rarefied (when, if ever, is it appropriate to begin a trill on the main note rather than the upper note? How long is an appoggiatura?). These and similar questions are the subject of much research among those who study surviving written music and compare it with what writers on music have to say about the meaning of written symbols and about the accepted conventions of performance.

At other times—and this is most frequent with older repertories—there are questions so basic that it's hard to believe that without a firm answer one could even begin to understand and perform the music. Such questions as "In troubadour song,

9

what is the rhythm of the melody?" or "Given that we have no instrumental music from before the thirteenth century, what are the instruments playing that are so often depicted in paintings and sculpture?" or "Why are medieval singers so often depicted with instruments if we have no written music for instrumental accompaniments to songs?"

In cases such as these, depending on your point of view, the music becomes a rich source for experimentation and expression, or else it is so distant that we cannot hope to produce a performance that would be recognized by the music's contemporaries.

The other aspect of early music, not so directly connected with performance, is an interest in musical repertories that have been rediscovered, in the sense that they were not part of the common coin of musical performance and experience. They have had to be found, either in surviving manuscripts, or in scholarly editions of the nineteenth and twentieth centuries—editions that were well known to musicologists but of little interest to anybody else. Sometimes it happens, for reasons that are hard to explain, that there is a sudden vogue for a particular kind of music—chant, say, or Vivaldi concerti for the violin or Bach harpsichord music. Some readers can probably remember such fashions—the "Chant" recording of the Monks of Santo Domingo de Silos (a compilation of old recordings from a Spanish monastery) that had a sudden and unexpected success in the 1980s; the surprising and persistent popularity of Vivaldi's "Four Seasons" concerti (I have never understood it); the popularity of (and recent revived interest in) the Bach recordings of Glenn Gould...not to speak of the so-called Pachelbel canon.

Historical revivals

There have been other times and places in which music of the past has been of interest. Various reasons can be given for these particular movements—often they are antiquarian curiosities;

sometimes they are the result of genuine artistic curiosity. Each is unique.

The last great work of the architect Palladio was the splendid theater of the learned academy of the Olimpici in the city of Vicenza, designed along classical Greek lines. Palladio died before the theater was completed, and the work was finished by Vincenzo Scamozzi. The theater was inaugurated on March 3, 1585, with a production of Sophocles' *Oedipus tyrannus*, in an Italian translation by one of the *accademici*, Orsalto Giustinian, with the choral sections set to music by Andrea Gabrieli. This was an attempt to provide for a modern audience a sense of the power of Greek tragedy, by having the choruses sung, as was done in ancient Greece.

1. **The Teatro Olimpico in Vicenza, Italy. The theater, designed by the architect Andrea Palladio, was made in imitation of classical theaters; it was inaugurated on March 3, 1585, with a play intending to capture the spirit of Greek drama, music by Andrea Gabrieli.**

In 1726 the Academy of Ancient Music was founded in London as a private club of singers, who met in a tavern to entertain themselves with vocal music; the first piece performed was a madrigal by Luca Marenzio. "Ancient" music was not music of antiquity but music old enough not to be in the modern repertory—what we would call early music. The members were well-known composers and singers; it was a gathering of professionals, with a few gifted amateurs (including William Hogarth); their programs always included Renaissance sacred music and madrigals, mostly by Italian composers.

A similar organization, called the "Concert of Antient Music," was founded in 1776; it gradually became a public concert series, performing music that was more than twenty years old; not very ancient, but it provided an interesting definition of early music in an age when almost all music was new, and when music rapidly fell out of fashion. Their concerts continued into the middle of the nineteenth century.

Gottfried Van Swieten, the personal physician to Empress Maria Theresa of Austria, was also director of the Imperial Library and had a variety of other bureaucratic posts. Van Swieten was a lover of music, and especially of the works of Bach and Handel, which he wanted to present to a wider Viennese public. "Every Sunday," wrote Mozart to his father, "I go at 12 o-clock to the Baron van Swieten, where nothing is played but Handel and Bach." Mozart was given the job of arranging Bach keyboard fugues for string trio (he composed wonderful introductions for them) to be played at these house concerts. Van Swieten also organized larger concerts, through his Society of the Associated (Gesellschaft der Associirten), giving full-scale performances of Handel oratorios in princely palaces, or the grand Imperial Library itself, or in the Burgtheater. For these concerts Mozart re-orchestrated Handel's *Messiah* and other works, adding parts for flutes, clarinets, bassoons, horns, and trombones, but respecting Handel's vocal and instrumental writing.

Even though the music of Bach and Handel was barely fifty years old (*Messiah* was first performed in 1742, Mozart's version in 1789), it was necessary to adapt it to modern Viennese taste, by providing appropriate instrumentation. Whether Van Swieten's efforts constituted an early-music revival or not, it is clear that he and his audiences appreciated the musical beauties of these two great—but outmoded—composers.

Beginning in nineteenth-century Germany, a desire to return to the true, authentic, appropriate music of the Roman Catholic Church produced a considerable revival of interest in the music of Palestrina as the gold standard for sacred music. Choirs were established on the model of Roman choirs of the Renaissance; editions of Palestrina's music were undertaken under the leadership of Franz Xaver Haberl (choirmaster of Regensburg Cathedral and founder of an influential music school). The ideas of *a cappella* performance, the avoidance of instruments except for the organ, and a musical style based on Palestrina's were characteristic of this international movement. Palestrina was viewed—incorrectly—as the savior of polyphonic music for his Pope Marcellus Mass, thought to have influenced the Council of Trent. A highly Romanticized view of Palestrina-worship is Hans Pfitzner's opera *Palestrina* (1915).

Although the movement was based in religious devotion, it also expressed a desire for an imagined artistic simplicity of the past--like the Pre-Raphaelites in England—and it reflected also the generally increasing historicizing museum culture of the nineteenth century.

One of the best-known moments of the revival of earlier music is the performance organized on March 11, 1829, of Bach's *Saint Matthew Passion* by the twenty-year-old Felix Mendelssohn. The performance was given in the Berlin Singakademie, which Mendelssohn knew well, having studied there and performed in the chorus.

His mother had given him a manuscript score of the work as a Christmas present in 1823, and he had studied the music from the age of fourteen. He convinced the director to allow him to organize a public performance, which would be the first time the work had been heard since Bach's lifetime.

Mendelssohn's version was hardly what we might now call "authentic." It was shortened, re-orchestrated, and the two choirs numbered several hundred. Wind instruments were placed at the back and extended outside three open doors. Mendelssohn stood between the choirs, with his back to one of them, and played on a piano from time to time; his conducting was occasional—he might start a section, and then stop gesturing once it was going well.

The performance was enormously influential. It led to the revival of interest in Bach's larger church works (his keyboard music never went completely out of fashion), and then to the foundation of the Bach Society (Bach-Gesellschaft), which produced a complete edition of his works.

Bach's music is far from Palestrina's (though he could write counterpoint as well as anybody); and the contrasting revivals of Bach and Palestrina, though they may both owe something to religious intention, seem also to have something to do with Romanticism, exoticism, and a desire for something real from a past that we have lost. Perhaps in the Bach revival there is also a sense of German pride at a time of rising nationalism.

In 1832, François-Joseph Fétis, the indefatigable writer on music, instituted a series of Concerts Historiques in Paris, mostly given at the Paris Conservatoire. He began with a history of opera, including excerpts from Jacopo Peri's *Euridice* and Monteverdi's *Orfeo*. The concerts were accompanied by lectures, which Fétis later printed in his *Revue musicale*. The concerts were long, and often not well performed, but they were well attended, and indicate that there was a certain curiosity about earlier music—

which the audience evidently did not know in advance. Fétis's approach was perhaps anti-evolutionary, in that music from the past was seen not as primitive predecessors of "real" modern music, but as a variety of fine styles.

So the revival of early music is no new thing. These and other moments in the past, however, took place at times that had in common the fact that all music was contemporary music; audiences and performers preferred new music to old. (This is not generally the case nowadays—we prefer music we already know, and we have a wide historical and cultural panorama from which to choose.)

In our own time, the wide choice of music we have makes early music only one of many possibilities that we can choose instead of contemporary art music. We do not normally think of our symphony orchestras as early-music ensembles, even though they play mostly music of the past. The early-music revival is self-consciously archaizing, in that it senses a gap, rather than a continuity, with the past.

We tend to group early music in broad historical periods: Medieval, Renaissance, Baroque. Indeed, the nineteenth century, as it recedes into the past, is rapidly becoming the subject of early-music revivals. Period-instrument orchestras now play not only Beethoven but also Brahms and Mahler. All music can be early music given enough time.

Chapter 2
Repertories: Medieval

The Middle Ages is the period usually defined as what comes between the end of classical antiquity and the rediscovery and revival of the classics in the Renaissance; for music, however, that period marks not a middle but the beginning of Western history. From Gregorian chant to the late fourteenth century, the music we consider medieval was among the first, and the last, to be revived in modern times. First, because the revival of Gregorian chant in the nineteenth century went along with the Romantic revival of Gothic architecture; and chant has been with us ever since, either as part of Roman Catholic worship or, increasingly, as concert music. And last, because in the recent revival of earlier repertories, Renaissance and Baroque music were more interesting, and perhaps more accessible, to those interested in earlier repertories.

There are many repertories of medieval music, most of them vocal. They include not only chant but great groups of vernacular monophonic song (troubadours, trouvères, Minnesang, cantigas, lauda); the monophonic and polyphonic embellishments of the medieval liturgy (tropes, sequences, conductus, motet, organum); the grand repertories of motets, sacred and secular, of the thirteenth and fourteenth centuries; and the polyphonic songs of Machaut, Landini, and their contemporaries.

All of these have been explored in recent times, and all present insuperable problems for the performer who requires specific performance instructions; for creative performers they provide challenges that some meet with more success than others.

Chant

In principle Gregorian chant has been around almost as long as Christianity. In fact, we know very little about its history before the first manuscripts of chant in the ninth century. Chant is the only repertory of Western music that is present throughout all periods of our musical history. It has never gone away, and so in a sense it is not early music at all, since it has a continuous and uninterrupted tradition. But it is in the nineteenth century that a sort of revival began, as churchmen and scholars sought to understand the early-medieval roots of this ancient song.

2. As a choir sings the leader points to the notes; the characteristic tapping on the shoulder to keep the rhythm is seen in many medieval illustrations.

The performance of chant is a complicated business, because the chant itself, and the ways of performing it, have changed considerably over the centuries. What may well have been a fluid, flexible style of singing—perhaps not unlike certain modern Middle Eastern sounds—is almost completely lost to us. The various ways in which chant was performed in the Middle Ages, the Renaissance, the Baroque, and modern eras is a remarkable panorama of changing style and taste. Whoever wants to achieve an "authentic" style of chant will have to specify a time and place, for there is no one way in which chant is sung.

Consider that the early notations of chant are intended to show the shape of the melodic line and some of its performance details, without specifying what the notes are or what their rhythm is. The notation we use today is predicated on the two factors that the earliest notation leaves out—the pitch and the duration; in modern notation, the performance nuances are either left out or added around the edges—indications of tempo, loudness, and the like. But the early chant notation is designed to remind rather than specify, and it includes some details we will never fully understand.

An example is a sign called a *quilisma*, a sort of wiggly line difficult to draw and surely having some performance significance; the quilisma is usually the middle one of three ascending notes; and when the early notations get transcribed onto a pitch-specific staff, the notes represented by the quilisma-figure are usually A-B-C or D-E-F—that is, the middle, quilisma-note is a half-step away from the next higher note. And the quilisma evidently wiggles: a ninth-century writer named Aurelian said that it had a trembling and rising sound, and the name itself in Greek means "a rolling." And in later sources, when many manuscripts write A-B-C, a few write A-C-C at the same place. It appears that the pitch of the quilisma is not obvious: either it is some sort of microtonal pitch, or it is a wavering, a trill, an alternation, of some

18

kind—a "trembling" between two or more notes. We will never know, and by the twelfth century some of these elegant performance-oriented signs (there are others also) had disappeared in favor of uniform single pitches. Imagine the difficulty of representing good jazz singers in notation, or trying to represent scat-singing five centuries from now without the benefit of recordings.

There was, of course, no uniform edition of chant (except for the efforts of some religious orders, like the Dominicans, to codify their books) until the early seventeenth century, when the printed "Medicean edition" (1614–15), compiled by Felice Anerio and Francesco Soriano, became a standard, much imitated through the nineteenth century. But that edition was a much revised and altered version of Gregorian chant, designed to late-Renaissance tastes, and by the time of Berlioz it is highly unlikely that any ninth-century Aurelian would recognize what was sung in Parisian churches as the same Gregorian chant.

A sort of early-music revival of chant took place at the monastery of Solesmes, established in an ancient priory in the 1830s. The

Chant performance in nineteenth-century Paris

Hector Berlioz was acquainted with Gregorian chant, and in 1830 he quoted the *Dies irae* from the Requiem Mass in his *Symphonie fantastique*. He seems also to have quoted the style of performance customary in Paris: long, even notes, accompanied by a strange instrument called a serpent (so called because that's what it looks like). Serpents were regular features of chant choirs in Paris at the time—Felix Mendelssohn in 1831 wrote, "In all of Paris you can hear no Sunday Mass that's not accompanied by serpents."

research carried out there, and the efforts made to convince the authorities of the Catholic Church that a return to early-medieval roots was indispensable, ultimately won the day, and the editions of Solesmes, and the official Vatican edition prepared by them, became the standard for Gregorian chant in the twentieth and twenty-first centuries. The Solesmes performance style, too, with its flexible rhythm and very smooth dynamics, became a sort of standard against which other performances are measured. The many recordings of the monks of Solesmes, made over almost a century, are enormously influential; they indicate, also, that even in a single place performing style changes over time, as the early recordings are quite a lot more robust than some of the later, Debussy-like singing.

Even though Gregorian chant is not much used today in the Catholic Church, there is now a thriving business in recordings and performances of chant. As concert music, as occasional music for special events, as music to relax to in a bathtub, chant has become a sort of musical symbol of the Middle Ages, and it has a life as concert music entirely divorced from its original purpose in the context of Christian worship.

Medieval religious culture emphasized anonymity and submission to tradition; the music of the chant is anonymous, and is fixed and immutable—or so it was considered. And yet the creative spirits of the later Middle Ages found ways to express their own artistic urges in various kinds of embellishments of the chant that allowed the chant to remain in some sense the same, while at the same time bearing new artistic expressions. We might consider these as horizontal and vertical embellishments; horizontal means that the embellishments are heard alongside the chant, before it as introductions, or during it as interpolations, and vertical means that the embellishments are heard at the same time as the chant. The first category is called troping, the second polyphony.

Tropes are poetical texts set to music and interpolated into a piece of Gregorian chant. If the Introit (the entrance chant of the mass) for Easter Sunday is "Resurrexi, et adhuc tecum sum" (I am arisen, and am with you), a trope might begin with a single cantor singing "Today brethren, the Lord is risen, and we all rejoice with the prophet who foretold this day, saying . . ." and then the choir begins the chant as usual, except that it has been introduced by the cantor in a sort of freeze-frame meditation. One or more times in the course of the chant, the cantor may interpolate further musical commentaries, and the choir simply pauses in its performance to hear the trope. It seemed perfectly suitable to chop up the chant into sections, provided that the whole chant eventually gets sung.

These musical and poetic commentaries—and there are thousands of them—open a window onto medieval meditation, and could be a rich source of musical material for early-music enthusiasts. Not many of them get performed, but perhaps there will be a vogue for tropes in the future.

One of the things that sets Western music apart from most other musical cultures is the extent to which we cultivate polyphony— that is, more than one note at a time. We have harmony, counterpoint, many-voice choirs, chord-playing instruments (guitars, keyboards, organs), and we take it all for granted. But the phenomenon is not to be found elsewhere; most other musical cultures cultivate a melodic and rhythmic complexity (think of the music of South India, for example) that far exceeds what we practice in the West: we have given ourselves over to the blandishments of harmony.

It began quite innocently in the Middle Ages, with the notion that the chant might be accompanied by a second singer singing the same chant at an interval's distance (as when men and women sing together in octaves, or when two people sing the same song but starting on a different note); or it might arise from two people singing different versions of the same song. We have a few notated examples of experiments of this kind, but it is easy to imagine that a lot of such singing never got written down.

What did get written is some highly developed repertories of polyphonic versions of Gregorian chant—music where the chant is sung, and *at the same time* one or more additional melodies are sung, in such a way that the chant has a sort of harmonic halo around it. One of the largest such repertories comes from the cathedral of Winchester in the eleventh century, in a form that cannot quite be deciphered; there are hundreds of chants, each of which has a second voice that sings the same words at the same time, but using different notes. We just can't quite tell what the notes are, though some modern scholars and performers have made very persuasive reconstructions.

A big breakthrough comes with the idea that you can sing *more than one note* for every note of the chant. This is the camel's nose under the tent, for it raises all sorts of possibilities that require coordination. When there was one note in the second voice for every note of the original chant—*punctus contra punctus*, or counterpoint—there were few problems of coordination: the chant got sung in the usual way, and the additional voice simply adopted the rhythm already well known from the chant. But when you have several notes in the additional voice (clearly you cannot alter the chant itself, or it will no longer be the chant), how does the chant singer know when to change notes? Either he will have to prolong some notes to accommodate the many notes in the other voice, or the other singer will have to go very fast when he has many notes, and slower when he has fewer. What is needed is a system of notating rhythm, and that is just what was invented.

The great repertory of polyphonic music from the Cathedral of Notre Dame in Paris in the twelfth and thirteenth centuries is one of the monuments of Western civilization, like the great cathedral in which it was sung. These pieces, called *organa*, were settings of chant, in which the choir sings the chant in unison, and, during the parts of the chant normally sung by a soloist, one or more additional voices accompany the original chant. In these pieces there are often many, many notes sung by the added voice or voices for every note of the chant, with the result that the notes of the chant are sometimes protracted to great length— there might be a hundred notes in each of two voices accompanying a single note of the chant. The result is, obviously, that the chant is barely recognizable—it becomes a series of very long notes, a foundation on which to erect a new and elaborate musical structure. Curiously to us, perhaps, it still seems that the chant is considered as being appropriately performed, even when it is unrecognizable to human ears—that is, after all, not its destination.

Sometimes in the course of an *organum* the chant speeds up, and the resulting lively *discant* style—in which all voices move in lively rhythm—became the source of a great deal of later music, written in imitation of those sections of church organa.

Indeed, some of these discant sections of organum became favorite source material for a sort of poetic practice of adding words to these long strings of notes in the added voice or voices. These words, originally of a sacred nature commenting on the subject of the chant, are rather like tropes, and could perhaps even be sung in the liturgy as part of the performance of the organum. But before long the same musical sections, extracted from the liturgy and cultivated as an art form, began to appear as short pieces of polyphony with Latin or, increasingly, French words with amorous texts; they were no longer suitable for church even though they were originally based on plainsong. These "worded" sections were named for their words: the French verb *moter*, "to word," has as past participle *moté*, or *motet*, and our word "motet" comes originally from the process of adding words to sections of a Parisian organum. The motet, as a genre, was a favorite musical and literary occupation of the thirteenth century, based always on a section of chant in one of the voices, with one or two additional voices, usually in French and usually on amorous subjects. But in the fourteenth century the motet became a major work, based still on a chant voice, but extending in size and complexity; such pieces were often written to commemorate political occasions or persons.

Song

People have always sung songs, but the only songs we have from the Middle Ages are those that somebody chose to write down. They are thus inevitably the product of literate people, or at least filtered through a literate culture. There is surely a lot missing. But what we do have is impressive in its beauty and variety.

Songs in every European language survive. There are Latin songs, some by students and other literate clerical folk at play—like the *Carmina burana*, a collection of songs (carmina) in a manuscript now at the monastery of Beuren (burana); extracts from its texts were formed into a choral work by the twentieth-century composer Carl Orff. The developing vernacular languages each have left a body of song; the troubadours of Old Occitan; the trouvères of Old French; the Minnesänger of Old German and their successors the Meistersinger. There are songs (cantigas) in Old Galician; sacred *laude* in Italian, and others.

Almost all the poetry of the medieval vernacular songs is strophic, and survives either in manuscripts of poetry alone or in sources that provide music. When there is music, it is music for the first strophe, evidently meant to be repeated for all the others. The music is generally written in the same notations used to notate Gregorian chant—that is, it provides no specific rhythmic information. Scholars have long argued, and indeed fought duels, over what the rhythm of medieval song was like, and it is a question whose answer will probably never be found.

In the fourteenth century there are traditions of polyphonic song, carrying on from the motets of the thirteenth century, that provide us some beautiful music, with specific notation that allows us to reconstruct the rhythms. The songs of Guillaume de Machaut in France, and of Jacopo da Bologna, Francesco usually called Landini, and others, in Italy, are a marvelous repertory of recoverable music.

3. An illustration from a Dutch astrological treatise shows a variety of medieval instruments: vielle, tambourine (with a snare), citole, hurdy-gurdy, and harp. The harp strings are incorrectly drawn; they should run from the pegs to the soundboard, not to the column.

Dance

Given the enormous number of references to minstrels playing instruments, and the pictures of individuals and groups of people playing instruments, and the instruments depicted in sculpture on church facades and elsewhere, why does so little instrumental music survive from the Middle Ages? The answer, surely, is that instrumental music was not normally written down. There are no music stands in any of those pictures.

We do have a few instrumental pieces: a small group of Italian dances, mostly called *istampitta* or *saltarello*, and a small group of French dances, mostly called *estampie*. Interestingly, each group is written in a different manuscript of songs, by not-too-accomplished hands in blank spaces in an earlier manuscript. They are essentially our only surviving dance music, and, except for a handful of keyboard pieces, and for a few isolated pieces and snippets that can be recovered from parts of motets and songs that may have been based on instrumental models, they are our only surviving medieval instrumental music.

There is something fishy about these two repertories—the very fact that they are written down. One wonders whether they are written because they are especially good examples, or especially difficult examples, of what they represent. Whether they are typical we will probably never know, but they are marvelous pieces, and without them modern medieval performing groups might be at a loss for anything to play. The dance pieces match a Latin description given by a Parisian writer, Johannes de Grocheio, of a dance called *stantipes* (a Latin word which corresponds to the French *estampie* and the Italian *istampitta* of the two surviving repertories just mentioned): formally they are like liturgical sequences, in that they consist of a series of units, each unit repeated with different endings; there might be seven such units, or more or fewer—but they all are repeated, first one way and then another. The music is monophonic, with rhythm clearly indicated; they are pieces, especially the Italian ones, that require real virtuosity to perform.

Performing medieval music

Performers of medieval music are faced with specific challenges—and with great opportunities. We know so little about how this music was performed that we can never be confident that we are doing something that the original hearers would recognize. On the other hand, the lack of information gives a very wide latitude for experimentation in which taste, rather than research, can be the only arbiter of success.

There are enormous problems: how do we perform the great organa of the Notre Dame school? Can anybody really sing the long notes of the chant while soloists sing the elaborate upper voices? Should we have several singers for the chant, staggering their breathing so that the note seems continuous? Should we add an instrument (the pieces are, after all, called *organum*)?

And what about the repertory of monophonic songs? There are so many pictures of singers with instruments, and so many references to composers and singers accompanying themselves on instruments, that it is hard to avoid trying to provide some sort of instrumental accompaniment or interlude; but the musical sources provide only a vocal melody in chant notation. From this, somehow, an instrumental accompaniment needs to be devised.

How? Perhaps by providing some sort of drone? Perhaps by using bits of the melody as introductions and interludes? Perhaps by playing on the instrument exactly what is being sung? Perhaps by improvising some sort of polyphonic instrumental accompaniment? All these methods, in various combinations, have been tried, with the result that an amazing variety of solutions can be derived from the same song. Probably the most performed monophonic song is "Can vei la lauzeta mover" ("When I see the lark") by the twelfth-century troubadour Bernart de Ventadorn; the many recordings of this song (by Russell Oberlin, Clemencic Consort, Early Music Quartet, Sinfonye, Paul Hillier, Gothic Voices, and many others) give a remarkable range of possibilities, from a single singer singing the verses to a multitude of improvising instruments.

Occasionally we get literary information that helps with performance. A song by the troubadour Raimbaut de Vacqueiras, called "Kalenda maya" (Mayday), is preceded by a description of how it was composed. Raimbault wrote it, according to the description, to fit the melody of an *estampida* he had heard played on fiddles by two French musicians. The song does have something of the form of an estampie as described by Johannes de Grocheio two centuries later, and if we believe the description, we can consider that "Kalenda maya" is the oldest surviving piece of medieval instrumental music. But what was the other fiddle player doing? "Kalenda maya" has been performed more times even than "Can vei la lauzeta mover," and it has become almost a challenge to think of something new to do with it.

Some performers have sought inspiration in living traditions of monophonic song, in North Africa, the Middle East, the Balkans, and elsewhere; perhaps such traditions are continuations of centuries-old performing styles.

The polyphonic songs of the fourteenth century present new issues. The Italian songs are sometimes in two voices, each of which has the same words—they can conveniently be performed by two singers. But what about the songs in three voices, where one of them lacks words; or the songs of Machaut in two or three voices of which only one has words? Are we to understand that the non-texted voices are to be played on instruments? Which instruments? Much controversy has arisen over this issue, and it may never be fully decided; the issue only gets stronger when we get to some of the beautiful songs of Binchois and Dufay in the fifteenth century.

Clearly the performance of medieval music is not a matter of reproducing what appears on the parchment but of finding a means of making it somehow come to life. The question of making it alive for modern hearers is an important challenge. The more interesting question—and the real matter of authenticity—is whether this modern performance would be recognizable and pleasurable to a medieval audience. That, alas, we will never know. We have modern audiences, and it is at least important to please *them*.

Chapter 3

Repertories: Renaissance

Renaissance, to musicians, means essentially the music of the fifteenth and sixteenth centuries. It is not really a rebirth of anything, but it is a period whose music has a sort of Apollonian balance; a quality found also in Renaissance visual art. This is the period of the great composers of polyphonic vocal music: Guillaume Dufay, Josquin Des Pres, Giovanni Pierluigi da Palestrina—all of them churchmen, at a time when church music was at the cutting edge of musical style (not so true today...). Masses and motets led the way for composers of other music, but all of these composers were also creators of secular song.

The fifteenth and, especially, the sixteenth centuries provide us with musical sources of a kind we do not have earlier: printed music. The printing of music is a complicated affair because of the coordination of words and music, and especially because the crossing of continuous staff-lines with separate note-stems makes setting individual characters very difficult. But from the very early sixteenth century we have beautifully made collections of masses, motets, songs, and instrumental music from the Italian printer Ottaviano Petrucci; his books were expensive, made by a time-consuming and difficult technique in which each sheet of paper goes through the press twice, once for the staves and again for the notes. By the 1530s, the French printer Pierre Attaingnant had developed a means of single-impression printing in which each note is provided with its own section of staff-lines. And through the sixteenth century a rising tide of printed music, sacred and secular, provides us a record of the range and extent of Renaissance music.

Sacred music

The sacred music of the Renaissance has never really left the repertories of church choirs. The Cecilian movement of the nineteenth century did a great deal to restore this music to the choral forces of cathedrals and major churches, and the cathedral and collegiate choirs of Great Britain have kept the tradition of Tudor church music alive in their enduring choral traditions. In a similar way, church organists have a continuing tradition of performing early music. But it is really the music of the late Renaissance—the music of Palestrina, Lassus, Byrd, Victoria, and many others—that is what we know and retain in our choral repertories.

Earlier Renaissance music—masses and motets of the fifteenth century, works of Guillaume Dufay, Josquin des Pres, Isaac, Mouton, Regis, and many others like the composers in the magnificent Eton Choirbook—do not lend themselves to performance by church choirs. The vocal ranges do not usually fit an SATB arrangement, the pieces have voices that do not seem normal (long-note *cantus firmus*, overly active parts), but they survive and revive on recordings and concert programs.

It is the professional ensembles, and not the church choirs, who perform and record the majority of the vocal music of the Renaissance. Most of these ensembles are not choirs per se, but ensembles of solo voices who most often sing the music with a single voice on each part. This seems, in fact, to be closer to the performance practice of most Renaissance performances than the treble-heavy cathedral choirs or the large university or church choirs of today. Much remains to be learned about the personnel

The papal choir, sings from the balcony inside the choir screen on the right wall.

4. An engraving of a papal ceremony in the Sistine Chapel by Etienne Duperac (1578; detail). The papal choir, gathered around a lectern, sings from the balcony inside the choir screen on the right wall.

of Renaissance churches and princely chapels, but it seems that even in cases where there are enough singers to double the singing parts, as in the Sistine Chapel, the singing was most often done by individual singers.

Sacred vocal music consists of masses and motets, with a few particular genres (hymns, sequences) that sometimes are also subsumed under the category of motet. A mass is, generally, a setting of the five sung portions of the Catholic Mass whose texts are invariable, and which can thus be named for their Greek or Latin texts: *Kyrie, Gloria, Credo, Sanctus, Agnus Dei*. Many Renaissance composers chose to compose settings of all five texts, often linked by some sort of thematic musical material.

In the fifteenth century, a favorite and much-admired device was to structure all five movements of a mass on the same *cantus firmus*. A cantus firmus is a pre-existent melody, often performed in long notes, and usually in the tenor voice (originally named for this function, *tenere* meaning "to hold" in Latin). It is clearly related to the medieval practice of embellishing the chant with additional voices while leaving the chant intact in one of the voices.

It might seem to make sense to use a chant Kyrie-melody as the cantus firmus of the Kyrie movement, a chant Gloria chant for the Gloria, and so on; and this is sometimes done: Guillaume de Machaut's fourteenth-century *Messe de Nostre Dame* is one of the best-known examples. But by the fifteenth century, it seems to be desirable to provide a sort of unity among the five movements by using the same cantus firmus for each; and in such a case, it is easy to see that a Kyrie-melody, though entirely appropriate for the Kyrie, does not make much sense for the other movements. And so it became customary to choose melodies from elsewhere: a sacred chant related to the subject of the mass (Dufay's masses *Ecce ancilla domini* and *Ave Regina caelorum* borrow the melodies of Gregorian antiphons; so do Josquin Des Pres's *Gaudeamus* and *Ave maris stella*; his *Pange lingua* uses a hymn). Various composers use a melisma (a long string of notes sung to a single syllable) sung on the word "Caput" in a Gregorian antiphon; many use secular melodies (Dufay has a mass *Se la face ay pale* based on his own song; Ockeghem uses song melodies in his masses *Au travail suis* and *De plus en plus*; Josquin composed masses based on *Malheur me bat* and *Fortuna desperata*; various composers, including even Palestrina, used a favorite song called "L'homme armé").

This tradition of the cantus-firmus mass is of enormous importance to composers and musicians in the fifteenth century; chief among them are Guillaume Du Fay (1397–1474), Johannes Ockeghem (ca. 1410–1497), and Josquin Des Pres (ca. 1450/1455–1521), along with his contemporaries Isaac, Obrecht, and Pierre de la Rue. The technique of cantus firmus addressed the challenge of providing both unity and variety in a long piece (such a mass was about as long as a Mozart symphony). The cantus firmus provided an underpinning against which the other voices could be composed; various sections where the cantus firmus is absent provide for duos and trios, often using the technique of canon or imitation; and the overall shape retains an element of unity.

Not all masses were based on cantus firmus technique, however. Ockeghem has masses with no cantus firmus: the mass *Mi-mi* (named for its modal character) and a mass *Cuiusvis toni*, that can be sung in any of several modes. Josquin has two masses based on canons.

Renaissance motets are sacred works based on Latin texts other than those of the Mass. Dufay composed a number of ceremonial motets in the grand cantus-firmus style of the late Middle Ages, but most composers assembled their motets using other techniques: sometimes *paraphrase*, in which one or more voices use the general outlines of a chant or other melody but adapt it to modern melodic style, or *imitation*, in which the voices enter progressively, each beginning with the same melody.

Imitation, familiar to us now from works of composers ranging from Josquin to Bach, Handel, and many others, is one of the chief contributions of Renaissance style. The technique is among the most important musical techniques of the sixteenth century and generally works as follows: one voice sings a motive, the next voice enters with the same motive while the first voice continues with new music; the third voice enters with the same motive while the other two continue, and so on until all voices are singing. There may then be a cadence, concluding a *point of imitation*. Or one of the voices may begin a new motive, imitated in turn by the others, probably in a different order this time, to make a second point of imitation. This technique has great advantages; it provides a sort of springboard cantus firmus, in which each entering voice sings the motive and provides a fixed point, a temporary cantus firmus, for the composition of the other voices. It also provides a sort of guarantee of the equality of the voices, since they all participate in the imitation. Variety of texture is provided by varying the number of voices; by providing sections in non-imitative counterpoint, or in homophonic style; by varying the imitation—imitation in pairs of voices, variation in the nature of the motive itself. Pre-eminent composers of sacred music in this imitative style include Palestrina, Byrd, Victoria, and Lassus: the composers whose music is often thought to represent the apogee of Renaissance church music.

Many of the masses, and sometimes the motets, of these composers of the sixteenth century, are based on pre-existent models (as were many masses of the fifteenth century). But for these composers the model is usually a polyphonic piece, a song, a motet, or a movement of a mass. The composer of the new work may use aspects of the model—its motives, its sequence of textures, some of its melodies—and recompose them to make an entirely new work. Palestrina's mass *Veni sponsa Christi*, for example, is based on his polyphonic motet *Veni sponsa Christi*; the motet, in turn, is based on the melody and text of a Gregorian antiphon.

Emulation of other composers, or of one's own work, was evidently an admirable quality; many composers used a melody by an admired teacher or contemporary in their own music: it was a way of showing respect.

Secular music

Not all Renaissance music was sacred. Songs, instrumental music for ensembles, and for solo keyboard or lute, account for the great richness and variety of genres and styles of secular music.

Vocal music for ensemble reached a remarkable high point in the Italian madrigal, which sought to give musical expression to poetry of the highest order. The various kinds of expression, from general emotions (grief, love) through individual descriptive details (birdsong, ripples, etc.), were among the delights of composer, singer, and audience. English-speakers will probably never fully come to appreciate the combination of literary and musical art that reached this zenith for Italians; but the madrigal was imported into England, and many examples were written there, inspired by Italian models.

Madrigal composers of the early sixteenth century were northerners working in Italy: Arcadelt, Verdelot, Willaert, Rore, and the younger Wert; later madrigalists were mostly native Italians: Andrea Gabrieli, Marenzio, Monteverdi, and the chromatically (and criminally) audacious Gesualdo. They set poems of Petrarch—the foremost source of madrigal texts—and also Ariosto, Tasso, Guarini ("The Faithful Shepherd"), and Marini, most of them great poets. The English madrigalists, however, did not set Shakespeare and his equals; their poems are more occasional and pastoral ("Phyllis gave me fairest flowers").

Madrigals are part-songs for groups of individual singers, and they are cultivated by the singers themselves, perhaps with a small audience; it is participatory music, available to any well-educated gentleman or lady. Later in the sixteenth century, as the expressive quality and the dramatic declamatory aspects of the madrigal came more to the fore, the pieces themselves got to be more difficult, requiring really expert singers, and creating the beginnings of a gap between music for the recreation of amateurs and music for entertainment by professionals. Dramatic madrigal cycles, "madrigal comedies," by such composers as Orazio Vecchi and Adriano Banchieri, linked a series of madrigals telling a story, assuming characters, and generally approaching a madrigal version of opera.

The gap between amateur and professional is an important aspect of the change of musical style, and of the place of music in society, that helps define the difference between Renaissance music and that of the Baroque period. Madrigals continued to be a source of recreation and pleasure, and they were among the first repertories to be "rediscovered" by the early-music movement; consider the Deller Consort, the editions made in England in the later nineteenth and early twentieth centuries, and the inevitable presence of a "madrigal" in Gilbert and Sullivan operettas.

There was plenty of other vocal music; madrigals were imitated in many other countries, but there were also simpler, more singable songs, designed for a single voice with accompaniment, or for several singers; often one of the voices would carry "the tune," the other voices assisting either as instrumental parts or as harmonizing voices.

The boundary between vocal and instrumental music was not so strict as we sometimes imagine. Music historians like to point out the "rise of instrumental music" in the Renaissance, and they are right to note the increasingly complex compositions for keyboard, lute, and consorts of instruments, a rich repertory of purpose-built instrumental music. But it remains true that the great majority of Renaissance instrumental music is simply vocal music played on instruments—masses, motets, madrigals, and songs played by instrumental ensembles—or versions of vocal music adapted for solo instruments ("intabulated" was their word, meaning put into tablature, or instrumental notation).

Renaissance instruments tend to perform in groups of like sound, a whole range of viols, for example, or recorders, from sopranino to contrabass, which can perform like a group of singers; such a group, or *consort*, could take on any vocal music that is within the ranges of the instruments. Composers enjoyed writing music for such combinations—the consort music for viols of Tudor England is among the great treasures of Renaissance music, even though the specific instruments are often not named—so as to provide maximum flexibility (and sales). Some publications are labeled as "apt for voices or viols," making evident what was standard practice for instruments. Sometimes instruments were specified, and when a mixture of instruments of different kinds played together (a "broken" or "mixed" consort) it might be the result of necessity, or it might be designed for a special sonority; Thomas Morley's book of consort lessons uses a standard grouping for late sixteenth-century England (violin or treble viol, flute or recorder, bass viol, lute, cittern, and bandora). Consorts of like instruments seem to have been the norm, rather like choirs of voices, but a household in which everyone played a different instrument could simply play whatever music was at hand, using the available musicians and their instruments.

A great deal of the Renaissance instrumentalist's time was devoted to providing accompaniments for songs. Many songs survive with lute accompaniments; sometimes these are newly composed, but often they are arrangements of madrigals, motets, or other

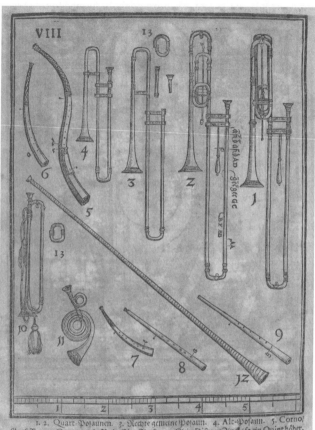

1. 2. Quart-Pojaunen. 3. Rechte gemeine Pojaun. 4. Alt-Pojaun. 5. Corno/
Groß Tenor-Cornet. 6. Recht Chor Zinck. 7. Klein Discant Zinck / so ein Quint höher.
8. Gerader Zinck mit ein Mundstück. 9. Still Zinck. 10. Trommet. 11. Jäger Trommet.
12. Hölzern Trommet. 13. Krumbbügel auff ein gantz Thon.

5. One of many plates from Michael Praetorius, *Syntagma musicum* (1619), which includes a Theatrum Instrumentorum (theater of instruments). These detailed illustrations give valuable information about instruments of the late sixteenth and early seventeenth centuries. This plate shows trombones, cornetti, and trumpets.

part-songs. It is an easy enough matter to create such arrangements on the spot: a consort might be formed to convert a motet or a madrigal into a song by having one of its voices sung and the others performed instrumentally.

The solo instrumental music of the Renaissance is a great and little-played treasure house of music for organ, harpsichord, and lute, and occasionally for solo melody instruments. The queen of instruments, and the instrument present in every Renaissance household, was the lute. There is an enormous amount of very artful and intricate music for lute, and the few lutenists in the world capable of playing it are worth seeking out and hearing. The lute is not very loud, and so it is not a candidate for Carnegie Hall. It is an intimate instrument, perfect for the player himself, or for a very few listeners, or for accompanying a singer (the volume of the lute may well say something about how singing technique worked in Renaissance music). Anyone lucky enough to hear works by Francesco da Milano (called "the divine Francesco") or John Dowland (whose lute music is of dazzling polyphonic complexity, and whose songs to the lute are unparalleled) will understand the heights to which the lute can lift us.

The surviving music for the lute is not all of this exquisite quality; there are many arrangements of vocal music, many of them skillfully done; lots of variations, dance pieces, and song accompaniments. And there is music for beginners; everybody learned to play the lute.

Music for harpsichord and other keyed instruments (spinet, virginal) is in many ways like lute music (you could even posit that a harpsichord is a mechanized lute), in that it consists of many intabulations of vocal music, lots of variations and dances, and a few pieces composed out of the fancy (as opposed to being based on something—a song, a tune for variations, a dance rhythm). These fancy-pieces—sometimes called fantasias, but with other names as well—are what the scholars point to as the "rise of instrumental music." And they can be grand pieces, some motet-like, some song-like, some dazzlingly virtuosic and improvisatory-sounding.

Music for organ naturally includes a good deal of music for liturgical use, often based on Gregorian chant melodies. There is much other music besides, in genres called fantasia, ricercare (often imitative like vocal motets), canzona (in imitation of French chansons), toccata ("touch-piece," which often sounds improvisatory) or, in Spain, tiento and ensalada.

The level of virtuosity in some of this music is very high. The *Fitzwilliam Virginal Book*, a very large manuscript book of keyboard music (so called because it is now in the Fitzwilliam Museum at the University of Cambridge), begins with a set of variations by John Bull that are so technically challenging that one eighteenth-century owner, the music historian Charles Burney, wrote that "some of these pieces, which were composed by Tallis, Bird, Giles Farnaby, Dr. Bull, and others, are so difficult, that it would be hardly possible to find a master in Europe who would undertake to play one of them at the end of a month's practice."

Improvised music

The music mentioned so far consists of the great repertories of vocal and instrumental music distributed by means of written copies and, in the sixteenth century, by means of the printing press. There is, however, a large body of Renaissance music that was never written down, because it was improvised on the spot. This music is of course lost to us, but it was an important part of the music heard, and we have some hints of how it was done. It is one of the great challenges facing modern performers to interpret and re-invigorate these important traditions. Three examples will have to serve for many.

In a manuscript book of organ music called the *Buxheimer Organ Book* (now in Munich), there is a great deal of music for liturgical services, most of it based on chant; there are also many intabulations of vocal music of all sorts, sacred and secular. A further element of the book's contents is the mid-fifteenth-century *Fundamentum organizandi* of Conrad Paumann, a blind organist in Nuremberg. The *Fundamentum* is a progressive textbook on how to improvise at the organ. Starting with what to do when the chant moves up one note, it progresses to what to do when the chant moves up a third, a fourth, and so forth. Then down one note, down a third, and the like. The idea is that you can learn to improvise an organ piece using any melody as a basis if you learn the simple rules.

Paumann's kind of music consists of a highly decorated upper voice, presumably played by the right hand, with the chant in long notes and a countertenor voice, these presumably played by some combination of left hand and pedals. There are in fact several versions of the *Fundamentum*, which must represent different stages in the teachings of this blind master—who must have dictated the various versions to different students.

The liturgical music in the Buxheim book and elsewhere make it clear that this style is just what is desired; the finished pieces in the book look like the result of the application of Paumann's principles. Anybody, then or now, who learned Paumann's system and who knew the notes of the chant to be interpreted, could be an endless source of new music without ever having to write any of it down.

The oldest printed book of instrumental music is called *L'art et instruction de bien dancer*, produced by a certain Michiel Thoulouze in Paris around 1496. It consists of a treatise on how to dance the stylish dance of the time, the *basse danse*, along with some music for dancing.

The music, though, is odd. Each dance consists of a series of square black notes, about thirty-five of them, with indications of

6. A late-fifteenth-century entertainment; couples dance the *basse danse* to music performed by a trio of shawms.

the series of choreographic steps. But surely playing thirty-five long notes is not very conducive to dancing.

As it happens, these melodies, or *tenors,* are meant to be the foundation for the dance (each note is the same length and corresponds to a choreographic unit), and also the foundation for a polyphonic performance of dance music. Musicians were expected to produce a lively accompanying part while a fellow instrumentalist performed the tenor. There are many pictures of instrumental ensembles consisting of a trombone (or perhaps a slide trumpet) and one or two shawms (loud, double-reed instruments) playing music (without music stands!) while couples perform the basse danse. In some of these pictures only one of the shawm players is playing. It seems that the alto shawm plays the tenor, and the shawm and the brass instrument provide counterpoints, one pausing for breath when the other player takes over. Occasionally the two players may perform simultaneously, especially perhaps if they are very skilled. Fortunately there survive a few examples of this music, in which a tenor in even notes—a tenor that corresponds to one of those in the Thoulouze book—is accompanied by one or two additional voices; these upper voices sometimes take turns, sometimes play together, but always have the same meter and rhythm—that of the dance itself. These few written pieces give us a valuable window onto a largely unwritten practice. It is clear that the instrumentalists for the basse danse do more or less what Conrad Paumann suggests: take a long-note melody and provide impromptu additional voices.

There are other sources of information about the basse dance—including a manuscript for the Burgundian court written on black parchment with gold and silver ink. The basse danse (sometimes paired with a livelier dance, about which we know less) was danced all over Europe, and traces of it are found in Germany, Spain, England, Italy, and elsewhere. It is the oldest dance that can be reconstructed with any degree of confidence.

Both the organ and basse-danse improvisations are concerned with adding additional melodies to a pre-existent chant or tune. There is another kind of Renaissance improvisation, very much akin to these in some ways, which is a system for making virtuoso instrumental music out of vocal music, but in this case the player takes an original vocal line and embellishes it by making many small notes for longer notes of the original melody. This process, called "divisions" or "diminutions" from the subdivision of longer notes into shorter ones, is described in a number of treatises from the sixteenth century designed to teach instrumentalists how to produce a virtuoso solo melodic line for their instrument.

One of the earliest, and the most musical, of these division tutors is the 1553 *Trattado de Glosas sobre Clausulas* of Diego Ortiz, a musician working at the Spanish court of Naples. His book is an instruction manual for players of the violón (presumably the viola da gamba). In its first part it gives ornamented versions of a variety of cadences and kinds of melodic motion (rather like Paumann's approach); and in a second book he gives a variety of model pieces, called *recercadas,* in several groups: a group of single melodies (solo pieces for viol); a group of six on a basse-danse tenor; a set of pieces on an Italian madrigal, and a set of pieces on a French chanson (these mostly ornament a single voice of the vocal model, with a keyboard accompaniment). Finally there is a series of recercadas on "Italian tenors," by which he means standard harmonic patterns (with names like *passamezzo, Romanesca,* etc.) that were well-known bases for improvised variations and dances.

These bass patterns are harmonic templates rather like the American blues, in that they consist of a standard series of harmonies that all musicians knew and could participate in; it would be enough, probably, to say "Passamezzo antico, in G, galliard rhythm" to set any group of Renaissance instrumentalists playing together, and to set any group of Renaissance ladies and gentlemen dancing.

Ortiz's treatise, however, and a number of others like it (mostly by Italians, including a professional cornetto-player from San Marco in Venice), are designed to teach something that in fact can not be taught, namely, how to be a dazzling virtuoso on your instrument, and how to take any song, or anything at all, and make of it a flashy showpiece. Some such virtuoso pieces exist in the written literature for lute, harpsichord, and organ, and mark the level of virtuosity that could be expected from the best players; but this virtuosity is not so readily seen in the literature for solo melody instruments—except as it is hinted at in this series of treatises on improvisation. It must have been a thrilling thing to hear a favorite song transformed in real time into an amazingly dazzling recorder solo. It's not unlike some aspects of jazz performance.

Performing Renaissance music

Renaissance music has a particular importance to the modern early-music revival. The perception of Renaissance music as participatory, the idea that there is a bridge between high and low culture, and the idea that music is accessible to all, are values that were important in this revival during the 1960s and 1970s. It is not insignificant that the most-wielded armaments of the movement are the recorder and the viol, and that groups of these instruments together, playing consort music, are the center of the many summer workshops and other gatherings that bring together performers at many levels. The Lute Society in the United Kingdom, the American Recorder Society, the Viola da Gamba Society of America, and their counterparts in other countries have done much to assure a continuing interest in the consort music of the Renaissance, and in the performance of vocal part-music on instruments.

The instruments used by modern amateur players to play Renaissance music are more or less Baroque instruments. Gambas of fifteenth- and sixteenth-century proportion are actually quite a bit smaller with respect to their pitch than are those—more of Baroque proportion—used by most players (this is actually a touchy matter: some experts contend that Renaissance viols were *larger*, but that only the smaller sizes have survived). Modern recorders, too—especially the remarkably good plastic ones—are mostly versions of seventeenth- or eighteenth-century models; Renaissance recorders have a different bore (meaning that these instruments are cylindrical rather than conical, as are Baroque instruments), and are not usually jointed. Details of this kind do make a difference in the sound, the agility, and the flexibility of the instruments involved—but only in the hands of experts; a good instrument in the hands of a good amateur can play a wide range of music, even if it is not the instrument that, say, Ortiz would recognize. Such a distance, of a century or so, is about the distance between Bach's harpsichord and Brahms's piano.

Other instruments are popular, too, among players of Renaissance instrumental music. The "buzzies," capped double-reed instruments like the crumhorn, the dulcian, the rankett (or "rackett"), provide a change of sonority, and sometimes an outburst of hilarity, when one of them is used or a consort is played together.

Some instruments are rarer, mostly because they can really only be managed by experts: cornetto, trombone, shawm: these are part of the "loud" category of instrument, generally used outdoors (shawm and trombone) or in church (cornetto, trombone) by professional musicians. There are some modern virtuosi on cornetto—likened by Marin Mersenne to a ray of sunlight in a darkened cathedral, and by others as the instrument nearest to the human voice—and there are a few ensembles specializing in loud-band music (shawms are very loud double-reed instruments). These give us something of the idea of what a Renaissance town band might have sounded like, or the kind of instrumental doubling or instrumental interludes to be found in some of the late-Renaissance works of church music by Giovanni Gabrieli, Monteverdi, and others.

In our time we have the good fortune to be able to enjoy Renaissance music in the way it was experienced in its own time:

from the Chapel Royal to the private household, the distance between professional and amateur, and the difference between their musics, was not so great that those who are listeners now might not be participants tomorrow. We too have splendid professional ensembles, and a thriving culture of individual participation.

Chapter 4
Repertories: Baroque

Passion, drama, rhetoric, gesture: these are the qualities that are common to Baroque art and to its music. The creation of opera was almost inevitable in an age that was so concerned with the expression of affective feelings, with heightened speech as a means of communicating passion. From Monteverdi to Handel, composers were in one way or another concerned largely with dramatic music; and even those who, like Bach, were not composers of opera, were nevertheless imbued with the rhetoric of the opera house.

Opera houses were the palaces of the people. In an age when Versailles was the model of a princely house, the creation of a public drama—for a paying audience—allowed for a kind of democratization of music that is surprising in the context of a time when a great deal of music was supported by aristocratic patronage. Princes had orchestras, some even had their own opera houses; and public concert rooms were very rare in the period. The church and the opera house were the most accessible venues for music. We admire the splendid festivals at Versailles, but we are more likely to have had access to the public opera houses of most of the cities of Europe.

Singing, dancing, and orchestral music are all available at the opera; and they were all translated for domestic use into cantatas, dance music of all kinds for the ballroom, and chamber music; the styles are similar, but the performing forces vary with the venue.

Opera, the characteristic new genre of the age, spanned the entire period and influenced almost all music, whether the music being composed was vocal or not—for opera, as musical drama came to be called, has all the defining elements of the style: acting, gesture, dramatic words, passionate language, all gathered into musical expression. A concerto by Vivaldi, a cantata by Bach, a harpsichord piece by Rameau, all share in the drama, the rhetoric, the passion of the stage.

The characteristics, and the forms, of opera are so pervasive in Baroque music that even those listeners who like only harpsichord music, or Bach concertos, or Handel oratorios, are listening to music affected by the dramatic and formal aspects of Baroque opera.

Baroque musical shapes

There are some essential characteristics of almost all Baroque music that give it its characteristic, almost instantly recognizable character. These include the expression of the emotions; the dramatic-rhetorical way of making a melody; the polarity of tune and bass line; and the dancing rhythms characteristic of most Baroque music.

Baroque music tends to have a single mood, a single intention, in each piece, expressed in part by a characteristic regular rhythm. Some call it the "affections," the idea that human emotions are directed and stirred by rhetoric, and that composers should do the same with their music. Embracing the belief that the four bodily humors (blood, phlegm, black bile, yellow bile) control our emotional balance, and that they allow us to shift from one emotional state to another only gradually, Baroque composers sought to express a single passion in each piece. In the case of vocal music, it is usually the emotion expressed by the words being sung; for instrumental music, it is up to the listener to receive the emotional message embedded in the music as interpreted by the musician.

The regularity to be found in many Baroque pieces is partly related to this desire for a consistent mood; it is also in many cases the result of a desire for dancing rhythms, or a constant rhythmic activity. It is one of the characteristics of this music, sometimes expressed by a firm regularity of the bass line, sometimes by a complex of rhythmic activity in the various voices of a polyphonic piece that taken together add up to a completely steady rhythmic flow. "Sewing-machine Baroque" is a term once used to describe the regular rhythmic patterning of a lot of Baroque music; but it sounds like a sewing machine only if you play it that way. The regularity is there, and it can be a joy.

Baroque dance music is found everywhere—in sonatas, concertos, keyboard suites, danced in opera, and sung as arias. Clearly recognizable dance rhythms are found in Bach's church cantatas, in his keyboard variations, in his preludes and fugues.

The stylized French dances that were an essential part of Baroque music, on the stage, in the ballroom, and in music for listening, were all cast in the same general "binary" form: a first part, usually cadencing in a secondary key, is immediately repeated; and a second part, beginning in that secondary key and ending in the home key is also repeated: AABB. But beyond that form, the characteristic meter and rhythm of individual dances is often so clear-cut that it takes only three or four notes before the experienced listener can say "minuet!" or "gavotte!" or "sarabande!"

Individual dances may appear anywhere; but a standard suite of dances tends to be arranged in an order that makes psychological sense; they are all in the same key, perhaps originally for reasons of tuning. A suite may or may not have an introductory piece: an overture, a prelude, or something of the sort (Bach's English

Suite and Partitas do have opening non-dance movement; the French Suites do not). Orchestral suites, often called Overtures, consist of an overture in the French manner (a solemn slow section followed by a lively imitative section), followed by a suite of dances.

Such a series, in the most common form, consists of the following order:

Allemande
Courante
Sarabande
["Galanterien"—optional additional dances]
Gigue

These dances all have Italian names as well: Allemanda, Corrente, Sarabanda, Giga. They are international in origin: German (allemande), Italian (courante), Spanish (sarabande), English (jig=gigue); but it is the French who put them all together.

Before the final gigue any number of additional dances can be inserted; here is where the composer puts his minuet, passepied, gavotte, bourrée, or whatever other form seems appropriate. Each dance has very strong characteristics: it would be tiresome to rehearse them all here, but a couple of examples may be useful.

Dances in triple meter include the slow sarabande, the moderate minuet, and the quick passepied. The sarabande often features an accent on the second of the three beats. The minuet is danced in groups of two measures which are often combined in hemiola rhythm (hemiola—"one and a half" in Greek—is the phenomenon of alternating, or superimposing, two triple units—two dotted quarter notes, say—with three duple units—three quarter notes; a good example is Leonard Bernstein's "I want to be in America"). The passepied is a quicker version of the minuet, but with an upbeat, often written in 3/8 or 6/8 time.

Melody, for Baroque composers, is prose, not poetry. It does not come in paired lines (like a folk song, or a Schubert Lied), but in rhetorical sentences or paragraphs. The essential melody is like a well-wrought phrase of Shakespeare or the King James Bible, consisting of an opening gesture, an amplification, and a close:

> When I was a child,
> I spake as a child,
> I understood as a child,
> I thought as a child;
> But when I became a man, I put away childish things (1 Corinthians 11).

A Baroque melody very often works like that: a *gesture*, or statement; an amplification, usually by way of *sequence*; and a conclusion, or *cadence*. (Music theorists sometimes use the German terms *Vordersatz-Fortspinnung-Epilog*.)

A sequence, in Baroque musical terms, is the repetition of a small musical phrase at progressively higher or lower pitch; it sounds complicated, but if you happen to know the Christmas carol that begins "Angels, we have heard on high," and then think of the long melody sung to the first syllable of "Glo......ria in excelsis Deo," you'll recognize that the music to the first syllable of "Gloria" has the same music sung three times, each time lower. That is a sequence; sequences may also be rising sequences; they may change key; they may involve just a melody, or the whole texture of a polyphonic piece. They are extremely useful for the amplification of an opening statement, especially when, as often happens, the sequence is often related to the opening statement by using its closing notes as the material of the sequence.

Perhaps that sounds complicated, but it is central to Baroque aesthetics. Ritornellos, those instrumental introductions whose recurrences shape so many Baroque compositions—are made this way; vocal phrases are made this way. The orchestral beginning of the chorus "And the Glory of the Lord," from Handel's *Messiah*, the vocal part of Handel's "Ev'ry valley shall be exalted," and the opening unison ritornello of Bach's D-minor harpsichord concerto, exemplify the technique. The sequences on "exalted" are a perfect example of the sequences that serve to amplify an opening statement ("Ev'ry valley").

The result of making music in this way is that it is like speaking in a sense. It is like an actor or an orator delivering well-wrought lines—it is theater.

The central aesthetic of Baroque music—and here I am perhaps on shaky ground with those who love Bach fugues for the organ and harpsichord—is the idea of a melody and its harmonic accompaniment. The focus on the drama of the melody is supported by the *basso continuo* ("continuous bass"), the chord-playing instrument or instruments that provide rhythmic and harmonic context.

This *basso continuo*, often shortened to "continuo," is an essential part of all Baroque music except for solo keyboard music and the very few pieces for an unaccompanied solo instrument (like the Bach suites and partitas for solo cello or violin—and even there it is implied). Composers indicated the rhythm and the chords of the continuo, not by writing everything out, but by giving the bass note of each new chord—thus giving the rhythm of the chords; the player or players knew what chord to play from seeing its bass note. When the composer wanted some chord other than the obvious one, this was indicated by numbers indicating intervals above the bass note, or a figure of some kind (a sharp-sign for a major chord, for example); this is why it is sometimes referred to as "figured bass."

Players improvised accompaniments, using the sequence of chords and the rhythm indicated. An organist will "realize" the continuo very differently from a lutenist: the organ can sustain a chord indefinitely at the same volume, but is not very effective at arpeggiated or rolled chords. Conversely, the lute is soft, and if it plays all the notes of a chord at once it will have a too-sharp attack and the sound will decay, so the player is likely to roll the chords to keep the sound alive (although a short sharp attack might be very useful if the singer were singing a word like "pierce" or "strike"). A harpsichordist will perform from the same bass-line differently from either. There is a great deal for the continuo player to think about, and one of the joys of playing Baroque music is to play continuo, for one is always making the music for the first time, and making every effort to respond to the meaning and expression of the melodic line, while taking account of other colleagues playing in the same continuo group.

The old idea of the "passepartout" continuo group of cello plus harpsichord (or organ for sacred music) has in recent years been enriched by many fine players of lute, Baroque guitar, chitarrone, lyra-viol, organ, harp, and many other instruments. The sound of a large competent continuo group is as satisfactory to a lover of Baroque music as the opening chord of *Das Rheingold* is to a Wagnerian.

Opera was itself a sort of early-music revival; at its origin it was an attempt to recover the affective power of classical tragedy. If ancient Greek characters sang their roles to the accompaniment of the *kithara,* actors who seek a similar effect should do the same: this idea led to sung drama, and to the invention of a new instrument, the *chitarrone,* to accompany the singers, and to a new reciting style, the *recitativo,* that turned imitation into invention. Thus a revival became the leading-edge artwork for the future.

It was Florentine humanists who were interested in recovering the tragedy of the ancient Greeks, and it was Florentines around 1600, Emilio de' Cavalieri, Jacopo Peri, Giulio Caccini, and others, who devised a means of singing roles in drama, to a fairly simple chordal accompaniment. And that is the origin of Baroque music. This is only a little bit of an overstatement: the focus on declamation, on drama, on rhetoric, on the one hand; on the other hand, the use of chords as a continuous accompaniment, a *basso continuo,* are the features, almost the only features, that are true throughout the long period of 1600 to 1750.

At its origin, in the early seventeenth century, opera is essentially a play, in which the characters happen to sing their parts instead of speaking them. This has always been true of opera, and it was there from the very beginning; the idea was that what we were hearing is *speaking,* not singing. This style of reciting, in the rhythm of the language, without all the repetitions of little phrases that would be true in a musical version, was called *stile recitativo,* recitative style. If you are not interested in what the characters are saying, in the elevated language in which they say it, you will likely be bored by recitative. But for the early Florentines, for Monteverdi in Mantua and Cavalli in Venice, and for many others, this style is what allows the literature of the play to be clear—and more than clear, expressive in the way that only melody can provide.

The recitative style began with opera itself, and the accompaniment provided for it was of the simplest. The *chittarrone* was devised to play appropriate chords to provide a background for the singer. A large, single-strung, lute-like instrument, the *chittarrone* is ideal for this purpose, and the revival of the *chittarrone* in recent years has done a great deal to help us understand the beauties of the early recitative style.

The earliest operas were sung in this style throughout; they were, it must be said, not especially rich in musical variety—but they were not *supposed* to be musical events, but dramatic ones, "authentic" revivals of the style of Classical antiquity: they were drama, they were literature. And if you were a literate Italian who

Ti caro caro Si   Ti Stringo   al fin cosi   Nel Seno amato

7. A performance of Handel's opera *Admeto*, 1727. This anonymous engraving caricatures two famous singers: Francesca Cuzzoni embraces the castrato Senesino as she sings, "Yes, beloved, yes, finally I embrace you thus, on the beloved breast." The engraving is on the title page of a printed letter claiming to be from Senesino to Cuzzoni.

did not know what to expect from opera, you probably found it absolutely delightful.

But not everybody found it delightful; there are those contemporary Italians who speak of the tedium of the recitative, and almost at once operas began to contain songs. It was easy to do: one of the characters invites another to sing a song, and he does so. (In some of the earliest operas, like Monteverdi's *Orfeo* (1607), the character who sings a song is the greatest singer of classical myth.) The problem is, of course, that if the characters are already singing, and we are to understand that singing in their world is the equivalent of speaking in ours, then how does a character sing a song? Again, it's easy: make it sound like a song: regular phrases, lively accompaniment, steady rhythm, and it's done.

The difference between song and speech, or aria and recitative, is a key characteristic of Baroque opera, and the relationship between the lyrical and the narrative has been one of the defining tensions in the whole history of opera.

Baroque opera is not a single thing, of course, but except for some of the very earliest operas, with a preponderance of recitative, opera comes to consist of a mixture of recitative and arias. By the late seventeenth century this became so codified that operas were almost as predictable in their form as other kinds of conventional forms that we adopt because they provide a focused pleasure: detective novels, or television situation comedies.

The form of a song in a Baroque opera is either ritornello or *da capo*. In the first case, there is an instrumental introduction that recurs at the end and throughout; in the second, the opening section of the song is repeated after a second, contrasting section.

Not all arias are like this, but there are thousands that are, and many others that are modified versions of it. There are two characteristic features: an instrumental ritornello that serves as a sort of refrain, and a breathing space for the singer (it also usually provides the singer's musical material); and a song that has a first part, a contrasting part, and a repetition of the opening. (In fact composers did not bother to write out the return; in a score it's enough to write up through Section B, and then just indicate *da capo*, "from the beginning," to remind the performers to repeat the ritornello-section.)

Why on earth would this form be so much used? Probably because it is so flexible, and because it provides everything a singer could want: an opening section, depicting some mood or state (anger, joy, sadness, longing); a second section that comments and amplifies; and then the chance to sing the first section again. This is in a way what the audience is waiting for—the repetition: it sounds different, first because it is now familiar; second because it

The *da capo* aria

In the standard Baroque *da capo* aria, the orchestra plays an introduction, called the *ritornello* because it will return. The singer then sings. The orchestra plays the ritornello again. The singer sings a new section that contrasts in key or in some interesting way with what she or he sang before; the orchestra plays the ritornello again. The singer sings the opening portion over again, probably in a varied or ornamented version, and the orchestra plays the ritornello for the last time. In sum:

Ritornello

    Section A

Ritornello

    Section B

Ritornello

    Section A

Ritornello

takes on a deeper meaning after the comment of the second section; and third because the singer jazzes it up with all sorts of flourishes.

The progress of an opera, at least of the classic high-Baroque Italian opera, composed and performed all over Europe, and imitated in oratorios, passions, and other kinds of vocal music, is fairly straightforward. The characters speak their parts, as in the earliest operas, in recitative style; now and then the plot advances to a point where one of the characters has an emotional moment worth pausing over. At that point, time stops, the orchestra begins to play, and the character comes downstage center, strikes an appropriate pose, and sings a passionate aria about how her character feels at this point, expressed in beautiful music. At the end we all applaud, the plot is usually arranged so that she makes an exit (provoking more applause), and then real time starts again with more recitative, until a character's situation is interesting enough to warrant another aria.

This alternation of real-time drama and freeze-frame commentary is the essence of Baroque opera; the recitative is there to get us to the next aria, and the arias are the reason for the whole thing. The plots may sometimes seem contrived or overly complex, but they are not intended to be realistic: they are meant to provide as many interesting emotional situations as possible, each one of which is explored in a characteristic aria.

Instrumental music

There are lovers of Baroque music who prefer instrumental music: they may not know much about opera; they may not much like the elaborate decoration that was the stock in trade of singers; they may not admire the plots of such pieces, or the seemingly interminable string of solo arias. And yet that operatic style informed almost all music, not just in the vocal sphere.

Baroque instrumental music can essentially be considered in two categories: solo (mostly keyboard) and ensemble music. Or it could be considered in two other categories: church and chamber music.

The essential instrumental genres are sonatas and concertos. A sonata may be for one instrument plus continuo (called a solo sonata), or two instruments and continuo (called a trio sonata— nobody is required to be consistent), or occasionally, for more instruments (quartets, etc). Sonatas tend to consist of several movements, alternating in character and tempo. Solo sonatas tend to be more virtuosic than trio sonatas.

A distinction between church and chamber is also evident in sonatas: a church sonata (*sonata da chiesa*) is a series of movements, in some order like *Grave—Allegro—Adagio—Vivace;* although they owe their origin to liturgical needs, it is clear that they were played for enjoyment in other places as well. A chamber sonata is essentially a suite of dances, each given its name. Suites of dances are familiar also from keyboard music and orchestral music; with chamber sonatas, however, the standard dance suite of the late Baroque—allemande, courante, sarabande, gigue, with optional extra dances before the gigue—was not so standardized. The dance form, however, and the idea of a series of dances, is the standard shape for a so-called chamber sonata.

The concerto has a somewhat complicated history. In the early years of the seventeenth century, especially in Italy and Germany, the term was applied to sacred vocal music for voices and instruments; Monteverdi used the word for his Seventh Book of Madrigals (which is actually a collection of pieces for voices and instruments), and Bach actually used the word sometimes for what we now call church cantatas. But mostly a concerto is a piece for orchestra with one or more solo instruments.

By the high Baroque period, the concerto came in two styles: the Roman type of Corelli and Handel, and the Venetian concerto of Vivaldi and Bach. Arcangelo Corelli, whose publications established the norms for solo sonatas and trio sonatas, also established a "type" for the concerto grosso in his Opus 6 concertos.

A Corelli concerto is essentially an amplified trio sonata; a group of two violins and continuo (called the *concertino*) plays continuously, and the larger group (the *concerto grosso*) plays occasionally, usually to emphasize beginnings and cadential moments. When the larger group does play, it plays the same music as is being played by the solo group—the orchestra is a sort of way of turning up the volume. Such concertos were wonderfully effective in larger spaces and were enormously influential on many composers; Handel is one of many composers whose concerti are modeled on Corelli's. Like his trio sonatas, Corelli's concerti (published 1714) are either "church" concerti, with several movements alternating slow and fast; or "chamber" concerti, presented as series of dances.

In Venice, the concerti of Antonio Vivaldi established another model, and one that was to be enormously influential. Vivaldi was not the first to compose concerti of this kind, but his influence was far greater than that of his predecessors.

There are two basic principles in a Vivaldi concerto that set it apart from the Corellian model: (1) separate music for solo and orchestra, and (2) the use of the ritornello principle.

They are very simple ideas, but very important. Consider a typical Vivaldi concerto (often a concerto for a single instrument; but there are hundreds of concerti by Vivaldi, for a variety of combinations of instruments—and not all of them are "typical"). The first movement begins with a characteristic opening ritornello by the orchestra (just as at the beginning of an aria in the opera house). Then the soloist or soloists (just like the singer) begins with new material. (Almost always the soloist also goes on to perform highly difficult music different from that of the orchestra and that contrast, of size versus agility, has been the backbone of the concerto ever since.) Sections of ritornello alternate with sections by the soloist, and the movement ends with a statement of the ritornello. Most Vivaldi concerti have three movements, with a slow movement in the middle; many second movements and finales have other formal shapes.

All of what is said here about Vivaldi concerti (and Corelli's for that matter) is highly generalized, and there are lots of exceptions. But it still holds true that those models were clearly understood elsewhere and were influential on composers all over Europe.

Johann Sebastian Bach's discovery of Vivaldi's Opus 3 concertos, called *L'Estro armonico* ("Poetic inspiration," 1711), was an acknowledged turning point in his life. He copied the concertos out in 1713–14 and transcribed some of them for organ, and his composing style changed forever: essentially what Bach learned was the use of the ritornello principle to structure the texture of a movement, and its larger form. His later music included a lot of concertos, including the famous six "Brandenburg" concertos; but Vivaldi's influence went much farther, and the ritornello principle was applied by Bach to movements in cantatas, passions, and many other genres.

Early Baroque music for keyboard, whether it be Italian, German, or French, can be played successfully on organ, harpsichord, or clavichord. Later composers tend to make more distinction between the organ (with its sustaining power, its colors and variety, and its pedals) and the harpsichord and clavichord.

Several lines of influence can be observed: the great Jan Pieterszoon Sweelinck in Amsterdam influenced composers in England, and also a series of North German composers: Scheidt, Scheidemann, later the great organist Dietrich Buxtehude, an important influence on Bach.

Girolamo Frescobaldi, organist of St. Peter's in Rome (he published two impressive collections of toccatas, capricci, and canzonas in 1626 and 1637, and a lot of liturgical music), was the teacher of Johann Jacob Froberger, the widely traveled court organist of Vienna. Froberger established the standard for the keyboard suite; his own suites were "rearranged" after his death (the printer, about 1697, moved the gigues that Froberger had usually placed before the sarabande and thereby established the pattern allemande-courante-sarabande-gigue). Froberger's music was influential not only on later German composers (Bach admired him) but also on the very important school of French keyboard composers.

French music for the harpsichord is a substantial and idiomatic repertory, drawing its inspiration from lute music and from dance patterns. Chambonnières, Louis Couperin (an admirer of Froberger), his nephew François Couperin "the Great," Rameau, and others produced characteristic pieces, arranged in suites called *ordres*, often with fanciful or descriptive titles.

The eclectic and unique Domenco Scarlatti, son of the Neapolitan composer Alessandro Scarlatti and harpsichordist to the king of Spain, produced hundreds of sonatas, mostly in the binary form used also for dances, that are dazzlingly inventive and idiomatic, and that had a profound influence on late-Baroque and later composers.

The keyboard works of Bach, like his instrumental and vocal works, are in a way a summary and a transcending of international styles of his time. His collections of suites (French and English suites, the Partitas) summarize a French tradition; the Italian Concerto and French Ouverture reference other traditions. Many of his collections are designed, at least in part, for teaching: the Inventions and Sinfonias, the Well-Tempered Clavier, the trio sonatas and the *Orgelbüchlein* for organ. The amazing Goldberg variations, the many concertos for harpsichord, all attest to Bach's amazing skill as a player, an improviser, a composer, and a teacher.

His organ music, more than half of it based on Lutheran chorales, is equally impressive and virtuosic. Including influences from other composers (Buxtehude, Pachelbel, Vivaldi, and others), his preludes and fugues, toccatas, and other independent pieces have been the proving ground for organ students, and the mainstay of the organ repertory, ever since the revival of interest in Bach's music in the nineteenth century.

The range of Baroque music

So far this section on Baroque repertory has dealt mostly with forms and genres, vocal and instrumental. Since Baroque music is so closely defined, in its own times, by conventions and categories, these are useful things to pass in review. It will be worth noting that a great deal of influence seems to come out of Italy and spread abroad. (In Renaissance music a lot of composers from elsewhere go to Italy.)

But not everything fits into the view of Baroque music we have just explored; what follows here is a series of remarks, or vignettes, of aspects of Baroque music that ought not to be overlooked.

The combination of Lutheran chorales from the Renaissance with the influence of Venetian sacred music of Gabrieli and Monteverdi made for a thrilling variety of sacred music in North Germany. Michael Praetorius (1571–1621), the enormously prolific writer and composer in Wolfenbüttel, discovered the new Italian style and speedily retrofitted much of his music to reflect the magnificent Venetian polychoral style, with basso continuo, ritornellos, embellished solo voices, and contrasting groups. He composed much new music in the style as well and made a marvelous combination of chorale and new style.

Heinrich Schütz (1585–1672), Kapellmeister at Dresden, was a student of Giovanni Gabrieli and deeply influenced by the music of Monteverdi (he made two separate trips to Italy). His *Sinfonie sacrae*, his *Kleine geistliche Concerte*, and other works, though they are not generally based on chorale melodies, brought the modern Italian style to Germany, and it spread widely through Schütz's fame, his printed works, and their quality.

A magical combination of French and Italian style, with a unique English quality, is found in the music of Henry Purcell (1659–1695), whose music for the theater is special for its quality, for its abundance, and for its brilliant setting of English texts. The so-called semi-operas of the London stage—spoken dramas with much music—included masterpieces of Purcell:

The Indian Queen, King Arthur, Diocletian, The Fairy Queen; his little opera *Dido and Aeneas*, though unfortunately incomplete, is a perpetual delight; and his sacred music, chamber music, keyboard music, all together make him one of the greatest English composers of all time.

The traditions of France have long been proudly different from those of other parts of Europe; even though opera was brought to France by an Italian (Giovanni Battista Lulli, later Jean-Baptiste Lully), the French version of Baroque music has many characteristics of its own, and was widely influential in its turn.

The operas of Lully and his successors, especially Jean-Philippe Rameau, do not follow the Italian model, but feature a much richer recitative, fewer showy arias, and lots and lots of dancing and instrumental music.

The highly stylized quality of French dance music, of French opera, of harpsichord and organ music, fits in well with the strictly codified style of acting and dancing on the stage. French style in all these matters, as well as in dress, literature, philosophy, and much else, were highly influential throughout Europe. The contrast of French and Italian style was one of the defining issues of Baroque music; even within France, the adherents of Italian music caused interminable arguments in the artistic and literary community about the relative merits of the two styles. Purcell, Bach, and many others owe much of their success to their skill in combining aspects of both styles in their music. Those who know Purcell's *Dido and Aeneas* will know a lot of French-inspired dance music, and will also know a classic Italian-style lament on a repeating bass line in Dido's famous "When I am laid in earth."

What's missing?

A chapter about Baroque music, about the repertories being rediscovered and reinterpreted, cannot mention everything. So far we have suggested the importance of categories, genres, and national styles, along with mention of some of the most famous composers. What we have *not* done is suggest the vast variety of music that is *not* by Corelli, Vivaldi, Purcell, Lully, Rameau, Bach, or Handel.

Many whole repertories, many fine composers, much music of high quality, remains to be discovered, performed, and recorded. This is one aspect of early music that is an important one, but in the case of Baroque music it has at times been overshadowed by that other theme of early music, the "authentic" performance of music perhaps already known. It is more dazzling to hear Handel's *Messiah* in a period performance for the first time than to hear some unknown piece, for the difference between one's accustomed version and the *new* early-music version is more striking for a piece one knows.

But there is a great deal of Baroque music waiting to be rediscovered. Marvelous things that we have not discussed include the Italian opera of the earlier seventeenth century (Cavalli, Cesti, Stradella); the underrated high Baroque German operas of Keiser, Hasse, and Graun; the virtuoso court music of Dresden, so admired by Bach; the richness of French opera apart from Lully and Rameau; the storehouse of French Baroque lute music of Denis Gaultier and others; the Spanish *zarzuela*. And much more.

Baroque music today

Baroque music is the keystone of the modern early-music revival, at least with respect to professional music making, just as Renaissance music is the key repertory for modern amateurs. The revival of the harpsichord was followed by other instruments that play Baroque music: gambas and recorders at first, in the hands of those who had already mastered the often less-challenging technical difficulties of Renaissance music, and only then the key instruments of the period, the voice and the violin.

Baroque music has never really been absent from the repertory; Handel's oratorios have never been out of favor, and Bach's keyboard music and his great passions and cantatas are the mainstays of performers, choruses, and orchestras. Church organists have never been far away from Bach's music. But performance styles changed over time, and the earlier styles of performance are what has been revived, along with some neglected repertories.

In the last decades of the twentieth century, however, the place of Baroque music shifted a bit. The early-music performers, recording in the 1970s, created a new world of Baroque music, partly by giving a new, airy sound to familiar pieces (Gustav Leonhardt's recording of the Brandenburg Concerti, Christopher Hogwood's of *Messiah,* various performances by Concentus Musicus Wien), and by bringing to our attention a vast number of pieces that had never been part of the repertory.

Since then, there has been continuing and increasing collaboration between the "standard" performing groups and the early-music world. Major orchestras program much less Baroque music, perhaps knowing that their setup and personnel are not really adapted for getting the best sound out of the music; and when they do perform Baroque works, their performing style is often informed by what they have learned from the early-music performers. Some orchestras invite distinguished leaders in the early-music field as guest conductors; some have Baroque ensembles drawn from their membership.

Early-music ensembles have achieved a level of expertise that makes their performances as inspiring and just as authoritative when they play Baroque music as those of the major orchestras when they play Brahms.

Chapter 5
Performing issues

An important aspect of early music, a way of defining it dynamically, is the effort to take a piece of music on its own terms, to perform music in its own way. If we grant that each piece of music comes into existence in a specific time and place, reflecting its own culture, then it follows that its audience was used to the musicians and the performing styles of that period. If we want to reflect that cultural background, if we want to have the sound-experience that listeners had when that piece was new, we should perform the piece in a manner consistent with other pieces in the same or similar style.

With the passage of time, performing styles change, musical desiderata change, instruments change. With the passage of a great deal of time, those things change a great deal; when an old piece is rediscovered, revived, and played by those much later musicians, and heard by those much later listeners, the result may be very satisfactory indeed, or it may not—but it will probably be different in many respects from how the hypothetical piece sounded when it was new.

Nobody—least of all early-music aficionados—says that modern performances on modern instruments with modern performing techniques, modern venues, and modern listeners, cannot be entirely satisfactory. What the early-music people *do* say, however, is that it would be awfully interesting to hear how Bach sounded to Bach, or Machaut to Machaut. Possibly some of the things that we do not fully understand, that do not quite seem convincing, will seem clearer when we have studied the performing techniques of the period; if we let the music speak for itself, in its own language, perhaps we will understand it better.

A great deal of research—in a field broadly known as "performance practice"—continues to add to our knowledge about the practices of past times. Instruments, playing and singing style, ornamentation, pitch, and tuning have been studied, discussed, and experimented with in recent decades. As we learn more, and as time and taste progress, styles change even within the early-music field. This is surely appropriate.

Where does early music stop?

This second approach to early music—taking the music on its own terms—is an attitude to performance that can essentially be applied to any music of the past—and almost all music *is* music of the past. The use of historical instruments and performing techniques has been applied far beyond Baroque music—the reconstruction of Mozart pianos, the improvising of cadenzas, Classical string quartets and orchestras played on period instruments, a Brahms *Requiem* with a Brahms orchestra and choir. And anything is possible in the future: a period-instrument *Rite of Spring* has been produced (hardly anybody uses F-trumpets nowadays, and the violas never play their instruments vertically in that arpeggiated passage in the Introduction).

The permeation of the "standard repertory" by early music, the use of historical instruments in post-Baroque music, is fascinating and has much to tell us; it is in a way delightful and sometimes shocking because we already know the music (or we think we do). It is an important part of the early-music universe, and one that surely would not be possible—given that this music has a living tradition of its own that believes itself to be authentic—had not the movement reached a stage of maturity and self-confidence that allows its practitioners to go head-to-head with major orchestras, string quartets, and opera companies.

The early-music revival got much of its impetus from curiosity about instruments no longer in use: clavichord, harpsichord, lute, recorder, viol. These, with the organ, were the first early instruments to be revived, starting in the early years of the twentieth century. It is on the basis of them that further efforts in the instrumental world were made—Baroque strings and winds, Baroque and Renaissance brass (trombone or sackbut, trumpet, cornetto, horn), Renaissance and medieval instruments of all kinds.

Organs had never gone out of use, but they had changed a great deal in the nineteenth century, developing into so-called symphonic organs of great power, and in the twentieth century, with the help of electricity, making a tremendous amount of variety and power available to a player who might be a considerable distance from the source of the sound. Explorations of the simple mechanical action of the organs of the seventeenth and eighteenth centuries, and their clear and bright sound, led to the rediscovery of existing old organs and efforts to reproduce the technical features, and the sounds, of the organs of the past.

Access to old instruments can be had in various ways. In some cases the original instruments survive—there are sixteenth-, seventeenth-, and eighteenth-century organs, harpsichords, wind instruments, and stringed instruments, among others. Some are in museums, others are discovered in antique shops, and others still, especially strings, have been altered to fit modern requirements and are still playing. Such instruments can tell us a great deal about how the old instruments looked, what materials they were made of, and how they were made. Such information can allow competent modern builders to re-create instruments that can help us to understand the music that was written for them.

There are paradoxes within the search for the right instruments. Harpsichords are reconstructed on the basis of existing instruments, but how do we know that the way they sound now is how they sounded to Couperin? Harpsichords were not made to be old, but to be up-to-date and new. Should we imitate the sound of an old harpsichord, or try to make one in original fashion and see how it sounds? If the results are different, which do we believe?

Problems arise even in those cases where old instruments are valued—particularly among the stringed instruments, where a Stradivarius violin is the *ne plus ultra* of modern violin players. In principle a Strad is a Baroque instrument; but many aspects of string construction have changed over time—pitch (requiring more tension on the string), neck length and angle (to play louder and higher notes, a longer fingerboard is needed, and that requires resetting the neck at a different angle), strings (gut has been replaced with steel), bow (the Baroque bow has given way to the Tourte bow, heavier and longer with more hair and more tension)—in search of more virtuosity and more volume. And to do all these things to a Strad requires it to be taken apart and braced much more strongly inside, and put together with a new longer neck and fingerboard, wire strings, higher pitch, and heavier bow—it is not at all evident that Stradivarius would recognize it.

Many issues have to be considered. One of them is whether it is appropriate to play on old instruments at all. There was a time in the middle of the twentieth century when it was thought desirable to "restore" old instruments to playing condition, so that we could learn from them. There then arose the view that every time you restore an instrument you lose evidence; after you have thrown the old harpsichord strings away, what do you do when somebody realizes that the alloys used, the string gauges compared to the pitch, have a lot to tell us about the sound? Restorers nowadays never throw anything away; but then there is often the question of which state of the instrument to restore it to.

In the making of new instruments, issues of various kinds, perhaps compromises, are inevitable. If a wind-instrument maker is producing copies of Baroque recorders or oboes, and if the instrument on which he models his new recorder does not sound at a pitch that matches any modern organ, harpsichord, or other instrument, the maker is likely to adjust the dimensions of the instrument so that it can play with other instruments. Doing so, however, runs the risk of altering the sound, subtly or not so subtly, by slightly altering the relationships or length, bore, finger holes, and so on. Lutes used to be strung with gut, where possible with the splendid "Venice catlines" that John Dowland admired. But gut is extremely sensitive to temperature and humidity, and a lute so strung risks perpetually going out of tune (Thomas Mace, in *Musick's Monument*, 1676, says that a lute player spends 60 percent of his time tuning and 40 percent playing). Nylon strings avoid this problem, and there are many lutenists playing on them—with surely some change in the resulting sound. How "authentic" is that? Harpsichords used to be quilled with bits of crow or turkey feathers; but as they are not as easily available as they once were from stationers, and since they break much more often, the harpsichord builders adopted a plastic called Delrin, which is widely used in harpsichords today; same question.

In general it seems that there are several stages in instrument building. First, the creation of something that is rather like an old instrument, but with all modern conveniences; Wanda Landowska's harpsichord, the so-called "Bach bow" (for playing the chords in Bach's solo violin music), the piccolo trumpet for playing high Baroque parts. Next comes the copying of original instruments, a stage of great importance, because it requires careful observation of what real-life instruments were like. There are indeed those builders who want the same wood, from the same side of the tree, and the same metal alloys, smelted in the old ways. And a third stage is one in which a builder has absorbed the skills and the competence to make the instrument; knowing how it's done, knowing the limits of appropriateness, and having an individual taste for the instrument, she can simply make recorders, or harpsichords, in the same free way as did the makers of other times.

Renaissance and medieval instruments can be more difficult to reconstruct. There are a few extant sixteenth-century instruments, fewer still from the fifteenth; since most musical instruments are made of wood and animal parts, they rarely survive long. For medieval fiddles, hurdy-gurdies, and some wind instruments, makers have to rely mostly on the visual evidence of pictures and sculptures. There are many, many, representations of musical instruments from the Middle Ages, often in the hands of angels or of the twenty-four elders who play around the throne of God (they are all playing rebecs on the façade of Wells Cathedral). What pictures and sculptures normally do not indicate is how the instrument is carved out and braced inside; what the strings are made of, how they are tuned, and especially *how they sound*. It requires some experimentation and some imagination to produce plausible instruments for medieval music.

We know that the pitch assigned to notes on the staff was essentially arbitrary for a long time. To a medieval or Renaissance musician the note "C" meant a note with a semitone below it and two whole tones above, in certain relationships to other notes. It did not mean a specific number of vibrations per second, as it does now. We know this from the fact that men's choirs and women's choirs used the same notation for medieval chant; we know it from the fact that in the Middle Ages the cantor whose job it was to begin a chant simply chose a suitable beginning note on the basis of how high and low the rest of the chant would go; we know it from the great variety of pitches produced by the same key on various surviving organs; we know it from the fact that the eighteenth-century flutist and composer Johann Joachim Quantz advises players to have a great many interchangeable middle joints of different lengths for their flutes, because you never know what the pitch of the harpsichord will be.

So how *does* one determine pitch, and does it matter? Well, it matters when instruments need to play together; if you travel to another city and find that the organ is pitched differently from the one you normally play with, you will either have to play in another key, or the organist will. For an instrumentalist, playing in another key can be extremely difficult, and for an organist it may result in some very out-of-tune sounds, since Renaissance and Baroque organs are tuned to play beautifully only in certain keys.

The pitches of instruments in the past can be determined in some cases. Original brass and woodwind instruments indicate their pitch by their lengths and other characteristics such as distance between finger holes, and usually we know where they were thought to be pitched. Surviving organs can tell us in the same way, by the length of their pipes in relation to the key that sounds them (there is a risk here, for many organ pipes are cone tuned—by mashing down or prying up the top of the pipes, and when the pipes get too messy the organ tuner simply retunes the organ by cutting off the tops of all the pipes). And occasionally there survives an old tuning fork (an instrument invented in 1711).

For the modern performance of early music, it is difficult to overcome these problems. Instrument makers began by making instruments at what has become a modern pitch standard (A=440 hz); but as they began to make more careful copies of instruments, it was found that Baroque instruments tend to be lower than their modern counterparts. Original instruments, and careful copies, do not all agree, of course, and after many discussions in the early-music world it was agreed, for ease of playing together, that modern "Baroque pitch" would be exactly a semitone below modern pitch (this was chosen to be fairly close to at least some versions of eighteenth-century pitch, and to make it possible for harpsichords and organs to participate by transposing the music down a semitone). It then became necessary for builders to make instruments to this standard, and harpsichord makers began to make "transposing" instruments, in which the whole keyboard could be shifted sideways to play at either modern or Baroque pitch. Some modern organ builders install an electronic dial device (transposer) to the console so the organist can play continuo for early instruments at whatever pitch they're tuned.

Naturally, some sort of standard is almost inevitable, so that people can play together, given that musicians nowadays do not live their whole lives in the same place and cannot simply have an instrument that matches the local organ. Since the adoption of "Baroque pitch" of A=415 (an equal-tempered semitone below the modern A=440), performers have been concerned that it is too broad a standard. Renaissance instruments generally play at a higher pitch, more like A=465 (modern makers do make instruments at this pitch); French Baroque orchestral and operatic music tends to be lower still, and many ensembles who play French music play at a pitch lower than A=415.

The level of pitch matters a great deal in other ways. Stringed instruments, which can retune by tightening or loosening their strings, will have a different sound if they play Stradivarius's instrument at A=440 than if they play the same music at a pitch much lower, nearer that for which the instrument was designed. Voices, too, find that the lowered tension of lower pitch has an effect on ease of vocal production, on how music lies in the voice, and on what sort of embellishment is possible. Playing music at a pitch near to that for which it was conceived—always remembering that the original pitch is seldom totally clear—can thus make a substantial difference to the performer and to the listener.

Pitch is one thing, and tuning is another. We now get into a fairly complex matter, having to do not with absolute pitch standards but with how one note relates to another. The word "temperament" in music refers to adjustments in the scale whereby some or all of the intervals are made impure.

A remarkable fact of physics is that the intervals we hear as most consonant are produced by small-whole-number ratios; an octave, for example C to C, is two notes vibrating in the proportion of 2:1; for a fifth, C to G for instance, the two notes are in the proportion 3:2; 4:3 generates a fourth, 5:4 a major third, and so on. The basic proportional scheme was known to the ancient Greeks and is the basis of a great deal of medieval musical and number theory. It sometimes helps to visualize a vibrating string pressed down at some point so that one side is twice as long as the other side; the two sides, in the proportion of 3:2, will produce two notes a fifth apart; changing the point of division can produce the other ratios. But there are complexities that require making adjustments, and the various kinds of adjustment produce a variety of temperaments.

A tuning system called "mean-tone" temperament was highly favored for keyboards and other instruments in sixteenth-, seventeenth-, and early eighteenth-century music. In this system some keys are far more consonant than they are in modern equal temperament (where all the intervals are equally out of tune); but others are almost unusable. The reason that all the pieces in a keyboard suite are in the same key, the reason that there are so few pieces in F-sharp major, is that the beautiful consonances of mean-tone temperament are in effect. Modern listeners at first notice something different about the sound, but it takes only a little time to understand the beauty of the harmonies.

Especially in the eighteenth century, various systems of adjusting tuning were introduced so that the most often used thirds were as pure as possible, but more keys were available for use. Names like Werckmeister, Kirnberger, and others, are

Temperament

In the matter of tuning things get very complicated very fast. Theoretically, if you took a series of twelve "perfect" fifths (C-G-D-A-E-B-F♯-C♯-G♯-D♯-A♯-E♯-B♯), you might think that the B-sharp at the end would be equivalent to a C, as it is on a modern piano. But this is not true, as computation and your ear will tell you. For the B-sharp to come out even with C, each of the intervals would have to be narrowed a tiny but noticeable amount. Indeed, this is how the modern piano is tuned—each fifth is a little bit narrow, so that all the semitones are the same distance apart, and all the octaves are pure. This is called *equal temperament*, because each of the intervals is altered—tempered—equally, and everything is equally a little bit out of tune.

This equal temperament is not how instruments were tuned in the past, and the various ways of dealing with the question of tuning has an influence on the sound of music. There is a direct relationship between tuning systems and the music for which they are used. Medieval music, to judge from the few instruments we have, and from descriptions of instruments, used what we call Pythagorean tuning (named for the reported discoverer of the proportions that govern intervals). In this system, intervals are pure: fourths and fifths are tuned without tempering; this is fine, but one result is that thirds, those intervals that we now think of as beautifully consonant (the first and third notes of "Mary had a little lamb" make a major third; the first two notes of "Greensleeves" make a minor third), are jarringly out of tune to our ears. But, in medieval composition, thirds were considered dissonant, and fourths and fifths were the "perfect consonances." There are places in medieval music—in the songs of Guillaume de Machaut, for example—where two voices pause and hold the interval of a major third. Machaut no doubt intended this to be dissonant, a moment of considerable tension; but to modern ears, and especially with modern tuning, it sounds rather mild and pleasant. In Pythagorean tuning, however, it is so jarring that nobody could doubt that this is dissonant.

A tuning system called "mean-tone" temperament was highly favored in the seventeenth and early eighteenth centuries. In this system some of the fifths are tempered more than others and are narrower even than the equal-tempered fifths that our modern ears are used to. This system had the advantage of making the most-used keys sound very beautifully in tune, with the special advantage of having major thirds, the definer of the key, also beautifully in tune. A disadvantage is that certain keys, and certain intervals, have to take up the slack, and these keys are so out of tune that they are almost unusable. It also has the disadvantage—or the advantage, really—that each "black note" of the keyboard, the sharps and flats (which are often white, or bone, or ivory, or wood, in Baroque instruments), can only be one note. That is, the note that stands between D and E can either be E-flat or it can be D-sharp—it cannot be both, as it is by compromise in modern tuning. If you want the other note, you have to retune the instrument. That is why certain keys sound awful; if you try to play in E-flat while the E-flat key is tuned to D-sharp, you will not like what you hear. (Actually, a few keyboard instrument makers got around this issue by making instruments with "split keys," in which the front part played D-sharp, while the back part played E-flat.) Another feature of mean-tone tuning is that the semitones are of different sizes (as, some think, they should be): diatonic semitones (D to E-flat, A to G-sharp) are larger than chromatic semitones (E to E-flat, G to G-sharp).

associated with various attempts to reconcile purity and flexibility. When Bach uses the title "Well-Tempered Clavier," he is not suggesting equal temperament per se, but the sort of temperament that allows all keys to be usable.

One of the beauties of these various temperaments (that is, those that are not the modern equal temperament), especially for listeners without perfect pitch, is that they allow each key to sound different. F major is not at all like A major; and the result can be that changes of key, distant harmonies, and surprising intervals, can have a dramatic and pungent effect not available in modern equal temperament.

All of this discussion of temperament and tuning is essentially focused on keyboard instruments, mostly because they are the instruments whose pitches are fixed. Singers surely were able to sing beautiful melodies, flexing the notes to indicate the difference between E-flat and D-sharp, say, without a temperament chart; and string and wind instruments tune to each other according to what the others are playing and according to the place of their note in the harmony. If keyboards were more flexible, perhaps these issues would never have arisen.

We have mentioned in various contexts that much early music has some element of improvisation or extempore ornamentation; the Renaissance instrumentalist, the basso continuo player, the opera singer, all are expected to be able to produce on-the-spot music never heard before. It is an important part of a great deal of early music, and has been the subject of much study.

The musical score that comes down to us does not represent what the listener will hear, in the same way that a modern piano or orchestral score attempts to represent everything that will happen in a performance. In earlier ways of writing music, the score is perhaps a set of suggestions for what might happen, a sort of fake book.

There are a great many examples of how the written music is meant to be used as a springboard for extempore music making. Most immediately present for most musicians is the constellation of little signs for ornaments that are to be found in French harpsichord music, and in French-style music throughout the Baroque era. J. S. Bach wrote out a table of ornament-signs and their interpretation, and so did many others. The French style seems to have been based on the idea of ornamenting an individual note with a trill, a neighbor, a slide, or many other possibilities. The French experts themselves make clear that the printed or written signs are intended for those who need that sort of guidance, but that an expert performer will use her own good taste to add others as well.

Italian Baroque music, by contrast, tends to ornament whole phrases instead of individual notes; the slow movement of an Italian sonata may consist of only a few long notes, and the performer is expected to use these as harmonic and melodic guideposts for an elaborate and highly ornamented solo melody.

We have already mentioned a number of examples in Renaissance music where performers normally make up their music as they go, based on conventional guidelines. These include the basse danse, in which one or more players improvise over a tenor of long notes; the organ-playing instructions of Conrad Paumann, teaching organists how to improvise using Gregorian chant tenors; and the divisions tutors, showing instrumentalists how to make a virtuoso solo out of a vocal melody.

There are of course many other examples: medieval vernacular song comes to us as simple vocal melodies, but the troubadours, trouvères, and minnesinger are so often depicted and described with instruments that we cannot help imagining that they accompanied themselves somehow while they sang. Unfortunately, we have no treatises explaining what it was they were doing.

What is clear is that much of the music we have needs to be interpreted in order for it to achieve the sound that it represents.

Performance requires a sense of style and a willingness to breathe life into the music.

Improvisation is not a matter of letting whimsy run free; it is almost always a matter of keeping within certain very specific guidelines (a jazz player would call it staying in the changes); a basse-danse melody, a specific chant, a pre-existent melody—the player always knows where he is and what the possibilities are and are not.

Particularly relevant to Renaissance vocal music, but much more widely applicable, is the composers' practice of expecting singers and instrumentalists to supply accidentals—sharps and flats—where appropriate, in the course of the performance of a melody. Much scholarly debate has raged about how exactly this should work, but essentially it is a means of ensuring consonant harmonies, and of approaching cadences in such a way as to make them effective.

Sharps and flats are found in surviving sources, but not always at the same places in two versions of the same piece. Performers are expected to be able to anticipate, and to adjust, their melody to the needs of the piece as a whole.

The great majority of surviving music from before the nineteenth century is vocal music, and the farther back in history we go, the higher the proportion of vocal music. And all of that vocal music is sung to words. It appears that in most cases the words are meant to be understood not only by the singer but also by the listener. They are words of religious importance, or words in a local language by a local poet.

There are perhaps a few cases where the words are not necessarily meant to be understood; the very long syllables of Notre-Dame organum; the multivoice motets, each with a different text, of the thirteenth and fourteenth centuries. But even in those cases, we either know what the words are in advance, or we understand that it is a piece to be admired in its construction—and even then, the words are available for visual inspection, and presumably at least the singer understands and hears them.

So the sound of the words is of primary importance. A performance that conveys the effect of the music's original state will have to take pronunciation into account. We know that language changes over time, and that the same vowel, the same word, is pronounced differently at different places and times.

In Handel's *Judas Maccabaeus*, even the paired and rhyming lines of his time do not rhyme today:

> Rejoice, O Judah, and in songs divine
> With cherubim and seraphim harmonious join.

Should we really sing "harmonious jine"? There are performers who have worked very hard on period pronunciation, in everything from Machaut to Dowland and beyond. The word "Sanctus," for example, sounds very different indeed with a nasal "n" and a French "u": when did French begin to make that sound? When did French begin to nasalize "m" and "n"? Linguists and others have given careful consideration to the history of pronunciation, and not a few musicians have made an effort to reproduce the sounds of language for the music of its time. Whether doing so is a good idea depends on whom you ask and on what you want to accomplish.

An equally heated issue is that of translation. Some will argue that music should be sung in its original language. Others disagree; a counterargument goes something like this: if we want modern audiences to experience the music as its intended audience did, they will need to understand what is being said—and thus meaning must take precedence over sound. As an English-speaking audience we can enjoy, and understand, the sounds of Dowland's language, of Shakespeare's, perhaps even of Chaucer's and of *Beowulf*. But in general we cannot understand Italian; if we are to enjoy a performance of Monteverdi's *Orfeo*, it will have to be sung in English. After all, its audience understood it as literature, they understood that they were going to a play in which the actors were to sing their parts, they knew the myth of Orpheus and were interested in this particular poet's skill in telling it in verse. Would not all that be missed if it were sung in the original Italian to a non-Italian audience?

It is easy to imagine the heated arguments that arise on this subject among very serious and committed performers. On the one hand, the music is composed with the sounds of the language in mind, with its articulations, its vowel sounds, its accentuation, its placement of expressive music at the point of expressive words—it is almost impossible to retain all these qualities in even the best translation.

And yet musicians throughout history have done so repeatedly; German minnesingers translated troubadour poetry; Monteverdi's madrigals were turned into sacred pieces; and on and on. This is an aspect of "authenticity" that will probably never be settled.

Given the preponderance of vocal music in earlier repertories, it is perhaps surprising that attention to singing came rather late in the early-music revival. This is not to say, of course, that early music was not sung until the 1960s and 1970s; there were always church choirs, Handel operas were occasionally presented, Gregorian chant was in use. But the instruments came first—recorders, viols, harpsichords, and then Baroque strings and winds. And along with the emergence of performing groups for medieval and Renaissance music, along with the revival of Baroque opera, came the question of whether the singing voice for medieval music should be the same as that for Baroque music and for Puccini.

There are those in the singing profession who believe that there is essentially one correct way to sing well; it has to do with support, diaphragm, larynx, breathing, vibrato, and many other technical matters. Many conservatories prepare singers for operatic performance, and their training is oriented toward the repertory of the modern opera house—the louder the better, with continuous vibrato.

Many early-music performers will suggest that, like other instruments, the voice is in a sense an instrument that changes with the times. There is of course no physical difference between the human organisms of the Middle Ages and the Renaissance and those of today, but if we believe that we can detect some sort of sound-ideal in the music of individual periods, we might conclude that the voice should be part of that sound-ideal. The trick is to figure out what it is and how singers could produce it.

One of the things, like tuning and whether to translate texts, that can provoke long and heated arguments, is the matter of vibrato. Is it or is it not true that vibrato is a natural part of the well-trained and well-employed singing voice?

This is not the place to answer the question; many people, especially singers and singing-teachers, will say yes. Here is how a counterargument might work. Consider the singers of South Indian classical music; they use their voices in an entirely different way from Western practice. They have a sort of high-larynx sound that no Western teacher would allow. Their vibrato can be regulated with respect to its speed, and with respect to the amplitude of its pitch-wobble, each aspect controllable separately, ranging from none of either ("straight" tone) to various amounts of each. If these aspects are completely under control by these singers, and they seem to suffer no ill effects from it, why should Western singers not be as much in control of their own voices? Some contemporary pop singers have this flexibility; they often use straight tone and add vibrato as an ornament.

Consider also the sounds of the Middle Ages. The instruments we know of are recorders, other wind instruments with finger holes, psalteries, stringed instruments with frets, all of which are instruments on which vibrato is either difficult or impossible (the same is true for a great many Renaissance instruments). If all the instruments sound one way, why would the voices sound different?

Modern string players also play with vibrato, almost continuously; this is possible on a fretless fingerboard by moving the left hand back and forth while the finger is on the string. We know that in Baroque music vibrato was considered an ornament, to be applied on occasion for expressive purposes; the presumption is that the rest of the time vibrato is not employed. Johann Joachim Quantz, giving advice to eighteenth-century orchestral players, warns them not to play with vibrato, since that is the privilege of the concerto soloist.

Some aspects of singing early music are difficult to reconstruct. Nobody seems to volunteer to become a castrato. The great voices of Senesino, Farinelli, and Guadagni made them superstars of an importance matching today's most famous rock stars. Castration of boys with promising voices before puberty was an Italian practice, arising probably from the prohibition of women's voices in church. By the late seventeenth century it became customary for the leading role in an opera to be taken by a castrato, and some of these voices are described as being of incredible beauty and power. Today, the castrato parts are sung by male altos or falsettists, or by women with voices of suitable range.

Reconstructing early music is challenging with respect to its sound. But there are also those who seek to understand the music more fully by understanding its role in performance: How did opera singers hold themselves, how did they gesture, how did they move on the stage? What did dancers do when a minuet was played? Scholarship and experimentation have added a great deal to our knowledge of historical gesture; especially in eighteenth-century France, clear categorization of acting and dancing styles, and their dissemination around Europe, make it possible to know a great deal about stage deportment.

Dancing manuals and choreographies survive from the mid-fifteenth century on, and scholars, dance historians, and performers have sought to reproduce period dance. When music and sight are combined, the result is to many spectators a rich amplification of a single stylistic period. Musicians who know how their music affects actors and dancers find that their performance takes on a deeper meaning.

The wish to re-create all aspects of performances in the past can lead to study of costume, of theater construction, of candle manufacture, of a variety of detail that can swamp the effort with trivialities. Room must be left for creativity, and drawing the line is always difficult.

The issue of authenticity

People sometimes object to the very idea of authenticity, and they make valid criticisms. The holier-than-thou (or more-authentic-than-thou) approach to early music can be exclusive in a not very useful way. The harpsichordist Wanda Landowska is often quoted as saying "You play Bach your way, I will play him Bach's way." In such a statement, there is the assumption that Landowska knows what Bach's way is; and there is the assumption that it is better for the performer to adhere to some external set of performance requirements than to participate personally in the performance.

Naturally it is not possible to know everything; we smile nowadays, perhaps, at Landowska's huge Pleyel harpsichord; at some of the mechanical, "sewing-machine Baroque" performances of the 1950s; at what perhaps was thought twenty years ago about the performance of fifteenth-century chansons. One wonders what will cause our successors to smile at us.

The conductor Sir Thomas Beecham recorded a commentary to go along with his recording of Handel's *Messiah*:

> During the past two hundred years, no great choral work has been played so frequently as Handel's *Messiah*. Yet it is safe to declare that during the last one hundred and fifty, there can not have been anywhere more than a handful of performances of full artistic integrity.

> There are two main reasons for this unfortunate fact: firstly, the general misunderstanding of the nature of Handel's music—a problem with which I do not here intend to deal; and secondly, the continued refusal, on the part of those responsible for the giving of his music, to observe Handel's own wishes respecting the conditions of its performance.

There speaks an early-music voice: we misunderstand Handel at our peril, and we should observe Handel's wishes. Beecham then goes on to say that, since in Handel's day choir and orchestra were about equal in size, he has chosen to double the size of his orchestra to match his gigantic choir. And thus he understands and observes Handel's wishes! (In fact, although the relative-size question is right, the numbers should be more twenty and twenty than two hundred and two hundred.)

We continue to learn from experience and from newly gathered information, but we are deceived if we think that everything we do is objective. If we really did it Bach's way, there would be nothing of ourselves in the matter, and the thing that mattered most to Bach, and probably to almost anybody else, is the presence of a musician.

What we may think of as the correct information is probably incomplete, and certainly arises from a comparative evaluation of a number of factors, each of which might be weighed differently by a different performer or listener, or in another cultural milieu.

What is authentic and historical to us may be laughable to someone else. The subjective is all around us.

The possession of the correct information is also a means of being exclusive: I know better, therefore my performance is better than yours. Who cares if you like it? This is the way it was at the time, and so you had just better learn to like it. Of course this is spurious, we cannot know for certain about most of these things. We do not know, for example, how an eighteenth-century harpsichord should sound, unless we have first listened to a number of them—and the first time we listen, we cannot expect to be able to judge the appropriateness of the sound. We do need to take the information as it comes, and make judgments only on the basis of substantial experience.

There are no period audiences; it will never be possible to give a performance of a piece from the past that will be received as it was when it was new. Too much has changed. It is possible to imagine places and times—Paris in 1198, Leipzig in 1723, Vienna in 1789—when listeners to music had a very clear idea of what they were about to hear and what it was likely to sound like. People in Vienna, for example, were extremely good at listening to symphonies and sonatas; Viennese music of the late eighteenth century was the only music they knew, and they knew it well. We have the privilege of access to a huge variety of music, but we will never acquire their expertise. We would probably not trade our breadth for their focus. We cannot unlisten to Wagner and Schoenberg, and we probably would not wish to do so, but it does color our listening to early music. It therefore seems reasonable to ask whether the attempt at an authentic or a historical performance is a thing achievable at all; we should perhaps do as Mozart did to Handel (and as Raymond Leppard did to Cavalli), and make it pleasant for modern listeners. That is, after all, what Glenn Gould did with Bach at the piano, and that is in fact what the early-music movement seems to undo.

Every moment is different, and the fact that no performance is the same as any other makes it clear that there cannot be an authentic performance in the sense of a definitive or normative performance. The nearest we can come to a repeatable performance is a recording. In many cases artists recording early music make a conscious effort not to be too spontaneous or novel or outrageous, knowing that what seems wonderfully quirky and expressive at a certain moment can be annoying when repeated endlessly.

A slavish reproduction cannot be a musical performance; it has no heart. If early-music performance is an attempt to get everything right, there is a sense that the very fact of attempting this will assure that nothing is right. The good performers know this, of course, and they attempt to assimilate a style to such an extent that they are simply playing music of a kind they know and like.

Richard Taruskin, in a paper first delivered at the Oberlin Conservatory and later published in a volume edited by Nicholas Kenyon called *Authenticity and Early Music* (and later revised and gathered into Taruskin's very interesting volume called *Text and Act*), made the canny argument that the early-music world's approach assumes that people are dirt. This conclusion was reached by his observing that early-music performers liken their activity to the cleaning and "restoration" of a painting in a museum—removing many layers of accumulated grime so as to see the original picture.

Likening the layers of grime to years of performance tradition, Taruskin wonders how one can so easily throw out the accumulated experience of so many people. Why would one want to do so? He is at pains to point out the mechanical performances of Stravinsky as exemplary of what early music *seems* to want, and he seeks to demonstrate the irreconcilable differences between the performances of the then-leading performers of the early-music world, Gustav Leonhardt and Nikolaus Harnoncourt. Although there has indeed been an element of earlier-than-thou—mostly among critics and audiences—there has seldom been real contention among serious performers, who both want to get at the essence of the music and respect its history.

In 1983, the scholar and performer Laurence Dreyfus published an article in *The Musical Quarterly* 69 (1983) titled "Early Music Defended Against Its Devotees: A Theory of Historical Performance in the Twentieth Century." He wonders why the early-music performance is an ethically superior one. He also posits that "Early Music signifies first of all people and only secondarily things," and notes that authenticity, whatever is meant by the term, is what cements it all together. Citing the social critic and philosopher Theodor W. Adorno, he notes that early music "fosters the attitude that subjectivity in interpretation…is irrelevant or, at best, unknowable." That is, early music pretends to an objective scientific approach that leaves no room for variability or subjectivity, and really believes that it can discover and reproduce the composer's intention.

In situating Adorno in his time, Dreyfus gives an amusing but accurate view of the state of early music in the 1950s:

> Adorno did not know Early Music as it blossomed in the late 1960s and 1970s but confronted the more barbaric gropings of the 1950s and a bit beyond. (He died in 1969.) This was the period of the "sewing-machine" style, sometimes called the "Vivaldi revival," when German chamber orchestras enthusiastically took up "terraced dynamics," when historically minded conductors urged players to stop "phrasing," and when repeat signs in the music occasioned a blaze of premeditated embellishments. "Motoric rhythms," it seemed, revealed a new species of musical gratification—the freedom from feeling. "Let the music speak for itself" was the battle cry. In practice: substitute brittle harpsichords for grandiloquent Steinways, pure Baroque organs for lush Romantic ones, cherubic choirboys for wobbly *prime donne*, intimate ensembles for overblown orchestras, the Urtext for

doctored editions, then one is true to Bach (or whomever) and his intentions. The musical results of this early purism were so sterile that we can hardly criticize Adorno for having missed the seeds of a critical new development.

Early Music seeks to reject the present, to repeat the past endlessly and to defamiliarize the familiar with new and unusual techniques. Producing novelty in familiar music is a means of avoiding the present while maintaining a semblance of something progressive.

Dreyfus, with only a little tongue in cheek, makes a comparative list of the social codes of early music and "mainstream" music, suggesting that early music makes every effort to avoid social distinctions and to repress the envy that results. He notes, however, that "the repression of envy leaves in its wake an enforced routine and a uniform mediocrity."

Here is Dreyfus's comparison:

Early Music	Musical Mainstream
1. The conductor is banished.	1. The conductor is the symbol of authority, stature, and social difference.
2. All members of the ensemble are equal.	2. The orchestra is organized in a hierarchy.
3. Ensemble members play a number of instruments, sometimes sing, and commonly exchange roles.	3. The "division of labor" is strictly defined, with one player per part.
4. Symptomatic grouping: the consort—like-minded members of a harmonious family.	4. Symptomatic grouping: the concerto-opposing forces struggling for control; later, the one against the many.
5. Virtuosity is not a set goal and is implicitly discouraged.	5. Virtuosity defines the professional.

6. Technical level of professionals is commonly mediocre.	6. Technical standards are high and competitive.
7. The audience (often amateurs) may play the same repertory at home.	7. The audience marvels at the technical demands of the repertory.
8. The audience identifies with the performers.	8. The audience idealizes the performers.
9. Programs are packed with homogeneous works and are often dull.	9. Programs contain contrasting items and are designed around a climax.
10. Critics report on the instruments, the composers, pieces and that "a good time was had by all."	10. Critics comment on the performer and his interpretation.

Laurence Dreyfus, "Early Music Defended Against Its Devotees: A Theory of Historical Performance in the Twentieth Century," *Musical Quarterly* 69 (1983): 297–322.

Performing issues

Early music as escapism, early music as socialism, early music as correction. There are many critiques, and many diagnoses of the ills and the advantages of early music as a "movement." But it is a movement, and that implies motion and change over time. When we consider something of how the situation came to be as it is, we can perhaps have a clearer view of the future.

Chapter 6
The modern early-music revival

The study of older music is characteristic of newer times. Why this should be so is a study more about modern culture than about music itself. Do we turn to the past because we prefer it to the present, like those in the Middle Ages who were convinced that the world was gradually deteriorating? Do we prefer music that seems somehow accessible to us, in that it is music that we ourselves might be able to play or sing, if we only worked at it a bit? (We certainly could not play, say, a Rachmaninoff piano concerto—the gulf between the technical abilities of professional and amateur is just too wide.)

Interest in music of the past is not a twentieth-century phenomenon, but earlier kinds of activities did not take hold of a large part of the musical world, since pre-twentieth-century audiences had very little interest in music that was not new. Nevertheless, the museum culture of the nineteenth century gave us some of our great collections of musical instruments and provoked interest in forgotten repertories; concert series, intended to instruct, were organized in several European cities. A number of significant composers participated in the edition of works by earlier composers: Saint-Saëns edited works of Rameau; Brahms edited Couperin; Webern edited Isaac.

Some earlier interests have led to enduring practices and institutions; examples include the persistent interest in

Handel's oratorios in nineteenth-century England; the nineteenth-century revival of Gregorian chant; the Cecilian movement that brought to life the music of Palestrina and others; the Schola Cantorum in Paris, a choir, later a school, for sacred music founded by Charles Bordes, Alexandre Guilmant, and Vincent D'Indy, which grew out of the series of concerts given by Bordes in the 1890s. All these and other trends have kept early music present to some extent, but it is in the twentieth century that early music, as a category, a kind of music, a movement, can really be identified.

A few significant figures in the twentieth century have had a great deal to do with the revival and performance of older music. Some are performers, some are instrument builders, and some are teachers, but all sought a kind of authenticity, a contact with the music that made no apologies, made no adjustments, and tried to hear it as those for whom it was intended might have heard it. That last is of course an impossible task—we cannot unlisten to the music of our own time in order to hear Bach with pure Baroque ears; and the seeking after "authenticity" has had its severe critics, some of whom we have met. But the splendid performances and recordings of these pioneers and subsequent practitioners have added enormously to the beauty and variety of the modern musical world.

Scholar-Performers

The beginnings of the modern early-music revival can perhaps be traced to Arnold Dolmetsch (1858–1940). An instrument maker, performer, and teacher, he was an ardent proponent of earlier music, instruments, and playing styles. His book on the performance of seventeenth- and eighteenth-century music, published in 1915, sought to be, and by many was believed to be, definitive. He made lutes, viols, recorders, clavichords, and harpsichords, played the bass viol, and from 1905 to 1911 ran a special department for harpsichords and clavichords at the

Chickering piano factory in Boston, Massachusetts. A friend of exquisites like William Morris and Isadora Duncan, Dolmetsch was fascinated with the physical beauty of early instruments; he made a name for himself as an authoritative maker and performer, and his school at Haslemere in England was renowned as a center for study and performance. The Haslemere Festival, begun in 1925, and the Dolmetsch Consort provided many years of concerts on tour and in Haslemere. The Dolmetsch Foundation continues in collaboration with members of the Dolmetsch family, sponsoring lectures, concerts, and summer workshops.

Among Dolmetsch's students was Robert Donington, a performer on the viol who taught for many years in the United States. His books summarizing and commenting on historical treatises were highly influential; they include *The Interpretation of Early Music* (1963) and *A Performer's Guide to Baroque Music* (1973).

Another effective scholar-performer was Thurston Dart, a widely recorded performer on harpsichord and clavichord, the editor of a great deal of music, and a prominent teacher at the universities of Cambridge and London. His little book *The Interpretation of Music* (1954) is a well-reasoned and deeply felt apology for early-music performance.

The composer Paul Hindemith founded the Yale Collegium Musicum, an ensemble of voices and early instruments, in the 1940s and early 1950s, giving concerts of music from the Middle Ages to the Baroque. A performer himself, his concerts, some of which were given in New York, were among the early efforts in America to bring this music before the general public. Hindemith had a special fondness as a composer for music that could be put to wide use, and for the complexities of counterpoint—both of which he found in much of the music of the past.

The American scholar Howard Mayer Brown (1930–93), who for many years directed a Collegium Musicum at the University of

Chicago, was a leading scholar of Renaissance music and of performance practice, and his support and encouragement of performance—not so common among scholars—and his many students and wide-ranging publications made him a major influence on early-music performers in America, even though he was not himself a touring and recording professional.

Medieval and Renaissance music

The early-music revival consisted of enthusiastic audiences and participants, eagerly absorbing recordings, concerts, and workshops and other teaching mechanisms. Especially in the realm of amateur instruments, mostly recorder and viol, the Renaissance repertory of consort music served as a wonderful entrée to the world of High Renaissance music. A number of viol consorts have revived and refreshed this wonderful repertory. The chief and most notable element of the revival of Renaissance—and to some extent also medieval—music is a series of mixed ensembles, performing mostly Renaissance music, and based mostly in England or America.

The American conductor Safford Cape (1906–73), who studied in Belgium from 1925, created and directed the Pro Musica Antiqua of Brussels, whose many recordings in the 1950s and 1960s were among the first to present older music of the Middle Ages and the Renaissance. A sort of all-purpose, multi-instrument ensemble, it performed a wide range of repertory in a style that seemed to be that of modern musicians playing competently. Only at a later stage would serious consideration be given not only to historical music but to performance techniques appropriate to the repertory at hand.

The New York Pro Musica Antiqua was founded in 1952 by the American scholar-performer Noah Greenberg (1919–66). This group assembled some of America's best performers of early music, many of whom were and are individually well known as

8. **Members of the New York Pro Musica in the 1950s. Noah Greenberg conducts.**

performers and teachers. The name "Antiqua" was later dropped
to avoid confusion with Safford Cape's ensemble. The many
recordings of this group and their tours (in which many
performers sang and played several instruments) provided a
model of sorts, what might be called the big-hardware model (lots
of impressive instruments), for how an early-music group could
operate. Ranging from Baroque music to medieval, the Pro

Musica was an important element in making a larger public aware of early music. They were insistent on performing in formal concert dress and avoiding the costumes and cuteness that Greenberg felt marred some other performance styles. With *The Play of Daniel*, premiered in New York in the 1957–58 season and later televised nationally, the Pro Musica made a spectacular hit of a (somewhat amplified) medieval liturgical drama. After Greenberg's death the group continued, with a series of other directors, until 1974; throughout the 1970s, many of the original Pro Musica musicians held summer workshops in early-music performance.

A different approach was taken by Thomas Binkley (1931–95), an American lutenist who in 1959 founded a group in Munich known later as the Early Music Quartet or the Studio der frühen Musik. This group of four fine musicians (Andrea von Ramm; Willard Cobb—later Nigel Rogers, later still Richard Levitt; Sterling Jones; and Binkley) made a specialty of focusing on specific repertoires such as fourteenth-century Italian song; or troubadour melody; or French *estampies*, and attempting to come to know them intimately, through exhaustive rehearsal. Observation and collaboration with Islamic musicians allowed the ensemble to incorporate elements that they believed might reproduce or simulate traditional medieval practice. Their international touring and more than forty recordings made an impact through the quality of their music, and through the contrast of their performances with the big-band Renaissance ensembles. In 1972 the group took up residence at the Schola Cantorum in Basel, where they trained many expert performers. Binkley later served as director of the Early Music Institute at Indiana University.

Musica Reservata, a London-based ensemble founded in the 1950s by Michael Morrow, came to prominence in the 1960s and 1970s with a distinctive approach to Renaissance music. A focused, highly directed sound (some called it harsh or piercing or screaming), based on observations of traditional singers, along with efforts at period pronunciation, improvisation, and attention to dance rhythms, kept the ensemble at the center of interest and conflict for a number of years. The remarkably flexible singer Jantina Noorman is particularly associated with this group. Some of their sounds were unusual and raised questions about the desirability of doing things that did not appeal to modern taste; others thought that taste is formed by familiarity, and that we should become familiar with the sounds, not just the notes, of older music.

David Munrow (1942–76), a charismatic and exuberant recorder player, founded the Early Music Consort of London in 1967; its performances and recordings brought a lively enthusiasm to a wide audience. Munrow's BBC radio series "Pied Piper" (1971–76) displayed his virtuosity and enthusiasm; his wide appeal can be measured by the outpourings of grief on news of his suicide at the age of thirty-three.

Anthony Rooley (b. 1944) was co-founder, with James Tyler, of the Consort of Musicke, based in London and centered on lute and viol. He expanded the personnel as needed for each program, working often with singers; especially associated with the group are the soprano Emma Kirkby and the bass David Thomas. Their recordings include complete surveys of the madrigals of Monteverdi and the vocal works of Dowland. Kirkby is especially associated with a nonvibrato, language-forward singing style, which communicates clearly and immediately.

A number of such all-round ensembles flourished also in America in the 1970s and '80s, many of them of very high quality; they include the Waverly Consort of New York; the Newberry Consort in Chicago; and the long-lived Boston Camerata.

More recent ensembles have tended to specialize more closely in a single period or style, seeking to expand their proficiency, their knowledge of a specific repertory, and their deep understanding of style. Among these are Sequentia (founded by Benjamin Bagby and Barbara Thornton in 1977, specializing in medieval monophony, with an extensive series of recordings of the twelfth-century mystic and composer Hildegard of Bingen); Mala Punica, directed by Pedro Memelsdorff, specializing in the complex music of the late fourteenth and early fifteenth centuries; and Piffaro, a Renaissance wind band based in Philadelphia. Specialist ensembles have the advantage of expertise, and in many cases of fleetness in comparison with the larger, all-purpose big-hardware ensembles.

Medieval and Renaissance vocal music continued uninterrupted, in a sense, in the Gregorian chant sung in Catholic countries and in the collegiate and cathedral choirs of the British Isles. Efforts to bring this music to a larger public in a concert setting was part of the same interest in early music that produced other ensembles, but the path here was somewhat different.

Recordings of Gregorian chant by the monks of Solesmes have been issued since the 1930s, and their singing style and their editions have been the standard for chant for a long time. Other monasteries and convents have also issued recordings. Since the Second Vatican Council and the abandonment of the Latin Mass, Gregorian chant is much less widely used in religious contexts. More recently it is heard most often in concert; performing and recording groups specializing in chant include Sequentia, Ensemble Organum, and many others.

Cecilian-movement polyphonic choirs existed in continental Europe, but more significant perhaps is the return to Tudor church music, spearheaded in England by Richard Terry, director of the choir of Westminster Cathedral, and the scholar and editor Edmund Fellowes in the early years of the twentieth century. A series of recordings of cathedral and college choirs on the Argo label in the 1960s and 1970s introduced many listeners to the beauties of English Renaissance sacred music.

Professional ensembles, such as Bruno Turner's all-male Pro Cantione Antiqua, led to a wider and nonliturgical appreciation of such music through recordings and concerts beginning in the 1970s; a similar group, undertaking Baroque choral works as well, is Harry Christophers' The Sixteen, founded in the 1970s. Alexander Blachly's Pomerium, founded in New York in 1972, is a mixed-voice ensemble that performs and records Renaissance music. The Tallis Scholars, founded in 1973 and directed by Peter Phillips, is today the leading such ensemble, attracting large and enthusiastic audiences; a flexible choral ensemble, it specializes in unaccompanied Renaissance polyphony and has a catalog of some thirty-five recordings.

Secular vocal music of the Renaissance was given strong support by the Deller Consort, led by the English countertenor Alfred Deller (1912–79), which introduced many audiences and record-buyers to the pleasures of English and Italian madrigals in the 1950s. The King's Singers, founded by choral scholars of King's College, Cambridge, in 1970, has included Renaissance vocal music in their extensive and popular programs; the long-lived group combines the sound of English choral tradition with close harmony, barbershop, and pop vocal styles.

The Hilliard Ensemble, founded in England by Paul Hillier in 1973, continues to perform vocal music of all periods, but is best known for recordings of medieval, Renaissance, and early Baroque music for unaccompanied voices.

Other vocal ensembles, like the Cardinall's Music (founded 1989 by Andrew Carwood and David Skinner and engaged among other things in recording the complete works of William Byrd), and the Clerks' Group (led by Edward Wickham) maintain a high standard and contribute to a wider repertoire.

A special place should be reserved for the female quartet Anonymous 4, which since their 1993 recording *An English*

Ladymass has attracted much attention to medieval music through this group's elegant singing style.

For many listeners, Baroque music is at the center of the early-music world, at least for concert and recording activity. In the case of Baroque music the issue around which much discussion revolved is less that of reviving forgotten repertoire than of de-familiarizing the familiar, applying nontraditional but arguably historical performing techniques to music that was already well known. Three recordings from the past serve to characterize the stunning changes that took place, and the three enormously important cities (Vienna, Amsterdam, London) in which a great deal of influential activity took place.

The first of these is the 1968 recording of Monteverdi's *L'Orfeo* by the Concentus Musicus Wien under the direction of Nikolaus Harnoncourt (b. 1929). A cellist by training, Harnoncourt founded this group in 1953 and with it, after several years of study and practice, recorded major Bach works, Monteverdi operas, and works of Telemann and Rameau. This recording of *L'Orfeo* was an eye-opening (ear-opening) experience for many listeners. The creative use of continuo accompaniment, the appropriate singing in the recitative style, the splendid array of late-Renaissance instrumental sonorities took a historical artifact that all music students knew about but few loved (there was then one very bad recording) and made of it something that changed the way many people felt about early opera and about Monteverdi. (Alan Curtis's 1967 recording of *L'Incoronazione di Poppea* has had a much smaller circulation.)

The second recording is Gustav Leonhardt's 1976 performances of the six Brandenburg Concertos. Harnoncourt had recorded them in 1964, but this recording was in a sense the summary of the accomplishments and the style of the early-music revival as practiced in Amsterdam. Not only was tuning and technique important in this style, but also a metrical sensitivity, a tendency to shape notes with a slight crescendo, and an effort at rhetorical phrasing. Leonhardt gathered around him musicians who were enormously accomplished and talented, each of whom was to be a leading teacher, artist, and performer.

Leonhardt himself (b. 1928) is perhaps the most important harpsichordist in the world and has trained generations of superb players. He studied at the Schola Cantorum in Basel, and in Vienna, where he also taught. From 1955 he taught in Amsterdam, and recorded and toured widely; he is especially fond of seventeenth-century music, especially Frescobaldi, Froberger, and Louis Couperin. He is early music's only movie star so far, having taken the role of Johann Sebastian Bach in Jean-Marie Straub's 1967 *Die Chronik der Anna Magdalena Bach*.

The Leonhardt Consort, with the addition of a stunning array of soloists, are the performers of the Brandenburg Concertos;

9. The harpsichordist and conductor Gustav Leonhardt appears as Johann Sebastian Bach in the 1968 film *The Chronicle of Anna Magdalena Bach* by Jean-Marie Straub and Danièle Huillet.

soloists included Frans Brüggen (then known as a virtuoso recorder-player, later as a conductor as well); Anner Bylsma, the wide-ranging virtuoso cellist; Sigiswald Kuijken, violin and viola (also now a conductor); his brother Wieland Kuijken (viola da gamba); a third brother, Bart Kuijken, is a leading flutist, but was not on this recording since Brüggen also plays flute.

Leonhardt and Harnoncourt joined forces on a mighty and significant project, the recording of all of J. S. Bach's cantatas. The series, in collaboration with a number of choirs (the choir of King's College Cambridge, the Tölzer Knabenchor, and others), allowed listeners for the first time to hear the enormous range and variety of Bach's church music, most of which, except for a few favorites, was seldom performed and mostly unrecorded. The series was begun in 1971 and finished in 1990; in the early LP versions, each recorded cantata was accompanied by the musical score. Since then others have traversed the complete Bach cantatas, most notably the Dutch keyboard virtuoso Ton Koopman (himself a student of Leonhardt) with the Amsterdam Baroque Orchestra in the 1990s, and the conductor John Eliot Gardiner's Bach Cantata Pilgrimage (1999–2004); the Bach Collegium Japan is bringing its own cycle to a close.

The third landmark recording is Christopher Hogwood's 1984 version of Handel's *Messiah*, with the Academy of Ancient Music and the choir of Christ Church, Oxford. In a sense it takes nerve to give the early-music treatment to what is perhaps the best known work of concert music, and Hogwood's lean, sprightly approach set many feet tapping and many heads shaking.

Hogwood's Academy was made up of many of the best players in a very active London early-music scene, which supplied musicians also for John Eliot Gardiner, Roger Norrington, Andrew Parrot, and many others. They staffed concerts, recordings, and many smaller groups, which performed chamber and more specialized repertory. London remains one of the most active venues for early music in Europe.

The French have always had a rather separate way with Baroque music—in the Baroque era and now. One of the important modern developments in early music in France was brought about by the American harpsichordist and conductor William Christie (b. 1944), who has been based in Paris since 1971 and, since 1979, has directed Les Arts Florissants, giving performances and recordings of French Baroque music (and much else). His presence and his art have stimulated much further activity in France, and there is now an active coterie of performers in France—many of them students and former collaborators of Christie's. They include Skip Sempé, Emmanuelle Haïm, Marc Minkowsky, and Christophe Rousset.

Since the 1970s there have grown up in cities both large and medium-sized a number of period-instrument orchestras, which operate as "shadow" orchestras of the local "mainstream" symphony orchestra: they have a regular roster, they give a season of concerts, they have a program of recording and touring. In many English-speaking places they give an annual series of performance of Handel's *Messiah*, which is to Baroque orchestras what *The Nutcracker* is to ballet companies.

Such orchestras are a treasure in their communities, and they provide the experience of hearing Baroque music in person—giving listeners the experience of the instruments (they are really quite a lot softer than the modern orchestra's) and the style. In each community, it is possible to revisit some of the great Baroque works: the Bach Passions, the Vivaldi concerti, and much else that becomes part of the standard Baroque repertory.

The Dutch violinist Sigiswald Kuijken founded La Petite Bande in 1972, having already played with the Alarius Ensemble for several years. He was the teacher of many of the players in London and elsewhere in the 1970s, so his significance is broad both as a performer, a teacher, and a conductor.

Of the orchestras with the longest standing, one should cite first those associated with London conductors: The Academy of Ancient Music (founded by Christopher Hogwood); the Orchestre Romantique et Révolutionnaire of John Eliot Gardiner (specializing in Beethoven, Berlioz, and Romantic music on period instruments); the English Concert of Trevor Pinnock; the London Classical Players (1978–97) of Roger Norrington; and the Orchestra of the Age of Enlightenment.

In North America, the Tafelmusik orchestra of Toronto has been directed by Jeanne Lamon for many years; the Handel and Haydn Society of Boston has in recent decades been constituted as a period-instrument orchestra (having been founded in 1815 as an amateur singing society); the Philharmonia Baroque Orchestra in San Francisco, directed by Nicholas McGegan; Apollo's Fire (Cleveland), directed by Jeannette Sorrell; the Seattle Baroque Orchestra directed by Ingrid Matthews; Boston Baroque, directed by Martin Pearlman. Many newer or shorter-lived efforts could also be cited.

In Europe, Ton Koopman's Amsterdam Baroque Orchestra has already been mentioned; newer Baroque groups, in Berlin, Venice, and elsewhere are continuing to provide stimulating recordings and concerts: the Akademie für Alte Music Berlin (1982), working largely in the former East Germany, has recorded many vocal works of Bach; the Freiburger Barockorchester (1987), a small group that also performs Schubert, Weber, and contemporary music; the Venice Baroque Orchestra (1997), founded by Andrea Marcon and specializing in Vivaldi and Venetian music.

There are a number of festivals, many taking place in the summer, that concentrate on early music. These are constellations of concerts, often by visiting artists, often concentrated on a theme, and usually including one or more large productions accompanied by concerts of smaller ensembles, workshops, and exhibitions. In Europe chief among them are the Flanders Festival (founded 1957), the Utrecht Festival, and the Regensburg Tage Alter Musik. In the British Isles, such festivals take place in York and Durham.

In the United States the chief such festival is the biennial Boston Early Music Festival, which centers on an operatic production, a series of festival-sponsored concerts, and a large group of independent events, along with a major exhibition of instruments, publishers, booksellers, and much else. Other festivals take place in Berkeley, Madison, Bloomington, and elsewhere.

An important role in the early-music movement has been the revival of instruments of the past. Much of the progress of the revival has been from hardware to software, from the instrument to how to play it, from the instrument to the voice, from the instrument to the world in which it was made and played.

The revival of musical instruments begins with the harpsichord and the recorder, and it progresses to the viol, the lute, other wind instruments, and Baroque strings. In all these areas, builders have changed over time from creating an instrument designed to seem familiar to modern players (recorders at modern pitch, harpsichords with pedals, lutes with frets) to instruments that progressively approach the look and the sound of the surviving historical instruments. For this gradual approximation, the great public collections of musical instruments have been of enormous importance.

Collections of musical instruments have many more purposes than providing instrument makers with models to copy. They preserve an important part of the world's heritage—and not only the heritage of European art music; they preserve the evidence of great artisanship and they preserve an important part of the historical social fabric. But to the extent that they provide access to the look, the sound, and the structure of period instruments, they have been enormously helpful, indeed crucial, in providing necessary information about the shape and sound of instruments.

Great collections of musical instruments include those at the Brussels Musical Instrument Museum, the Musikinstrumenten-Museum Berlin, the Sammlung alter Musikinstrumente Vienna, the Paris Conservatoire (now the Musée de la Musique), the Bate Collection at Oxford, the University of Edinburgh, and the Horniman Museum in London. In the United States, the Museum of Fine Arts, Boston, the Metropolitan Museum in New York, Yale University, the Smithsonian Institution in Washington, and the National Music Museum in Vermilion, South Dakota, hold the leading collections. Some of these, but especially the Smithsonian Institution, have active concert seasons associated with the instruments.

Museum policy varies from place to place, but generally over the last decades there has been a shift from the practice of restoring instruments to playing condition to a practice of stabilizing instruments but leaving them more or less as they are found. This latter process preserves as much historical information as possible, but there are those who lament the absence of the sound itself as the most important information of all.

Such collections, in providing access, measurements, and drawings to instrument builders, have enabled builders wishing to proceed on historical principles to model their instruments on a range of surviving copies. This works best, of course, for more recent instruments. From the eighteenth and nineteenth centuries a relatively large number of instruments survives; from the seventeenth century and earlier there are fewer and fewer extant instruments until the repertory of medieval instruments is reduced to essentially a few bone flutes and ceremonial ivory trumpets.

With respect to the harpsichord—the symbolic early instrument in the early years of the twentieth century—the instrument was "revived" by players like Wanda Landowska, who wished to play on appropriate instruments for Bach and Rameau. The instruments of Pleyel, of John Challis, of the German series-builders Neupert, Wittmayer, and Sperrhake made instruments available, but they were instruments designed to meet certain modern goals: volume, stability, ease of register-shifting.

Arnold Dolmetsch, working in England and in the United States, gave serious attention to harpsichords, clavichords, lutes, and viols, and made extensive efforts to make instruments that reflected historical models.

In 1949 the American builders Frank Hubbard and William Dowd (who had been apprentices to John Challis, who had studied with Dolmetsch) began—first together, and then in separate shops—to make historically oriented harpsichords, as did other builders in England and on the Continent, such as Martin Skowroneck in Bremen. Today, there is a wide range of harpsichords available, representing many historical periods, many national traditions, and many styles of manufacture. One particular phenomenon of interest is the "kit" harpsichord, in which a maker like Zuckermann or Hubbard provides a series of pre-cut parts and a series of drawings, leaving it to the customer to finish the instrument; the results range with the artisanal skill of the buyer.

There was a great deal more to do than rebuild harpsichords. A large part of how early music sounds in the present, and how successfully it is executed depends, for better or worse, on the skills of builders of recorders, strings, winds, brass, and organs. The work done on restoring old instruments, and figuring out how they worked, laid the groundwork for builders of modern copies in many areas.

Makers of fine recorders are sometimes also the makers of cheap instruments, and there are on the market some bad, but some rather good, plastic instruments, which in the hands of beginners or of children can be an economical path of access to music.

Musical instrument collectors and their associations have some relationship to early music, although such groups also include collectors of Theremins, synthesizers, and the like. The Galpin Society in England and the American Musical Instrument Society have meetings, publish distinguished journals, and provide means of contact among collectors, dealers, and aficionados.

The history of soloists and ensembles is essentially a tale of professionals playing for amateurs. But a significant aspect of the early-music movement is the participatory aspect: this is, for many, a type of music that one can play and sing rather easily. And it is organized in a sort of grass-roots, nonhierarchical network of training and playing opportunities that lie largely outside traditional concert and educational structures—or it did so in the 1970s and 1980s, when this aspect of the movement was at its height.

From the Dolmetsch workshops on, there have been playing and training courses, many taking place in the summer, that allow amateurs to learn an instrument, to sing and play in ensembles at an appropriate level, and especially to enjoy music making. There are countless summer workshops, many of which attract essentially the same group of eager participants year after year. Some are focused on a single instrument—usually recorder or viol (sometimes having an expert course alongside); others on a repertory or style, like the Oberlin Baroque Performance Institute (which caters to pre-professionals); others still have many facets, like the Amherst Early Music courses in the United States.

There may be reason to believe that the essentially participatory aspect of early music was at its most attractive in the 1960s and 1970s, at a time when folk music, hippie culture, and antiwar counterculture activities were at their height. Participation in

10. Amateur performers at the annual Amherst Early Music summer workshop.

early music was being part of a nonhierarchical world, in which each player has her important part, there is no conductor, there is no distinction between professional and amateur, and the activity is refreshing and free. There was a sense, too, that the organization of workshops outside of the traditional educational structures was part of the creation of an alternative society, one in which skill rather than diplomas, patience rather than discipline, informality rather than bureaucracy were supported and valued.

A sense of common exploration, of figuring out how this music works, how these instruments sound best, and discovering new repertoire were attractive aspects of participation in early music; one did not make slavish imitations of a teacher who knew exactly how any piece in a restricted repertory ought to go. The concept was that we are all in this together, and we are learning as we go.

It appears, from the increasing average age of the membership of such groups as the American Recorder Society and the Gamba Society, that the attraction of early music as a world of equality and collaboration is not as strong for the young people of today as it was for their elders.

In 1989, the national service organization Early Music America conducted a survey of its members and of members of other early-music associations; of those surveyed who considered themselves musicians, either professional or amateur, a large proportion reported that they acquired their skills either privately from a teacher or from early-music workshops—not, that is, through traditional music school or conservatory training. I expect that the proportion would be considerably lower today.

Professionalization: training

Early music has gradually taken a place in the professional musical world of training, performing, and recording. From the time of Bach and before, university students gathered in a Collegium Musicum to perform music together. German universities have had such organizations in modern times, including those of Riemann in Leipzig (1908), Gurlitt in Freiburg (1920s), and Hindemith at Yale (1940s).

In American universities, and in many others as well, there is very often one or more early-music groups, often called Collegium Musicum. Such groups are sometimes associated with courses in the history of music; sometimes they are vocal ensembles, more often a multi-instrument, all-purpose Renaissance ensemble; in some cases a variety of ensembles—viols, recorders, winds, voices—are part of a larger organization. The level of competence in these ensembles varies considerably. Sometimes they are recreational activities, granting no academic credit, and recruiting from students and the community at large; participants sometimes begin by learning to play the instruments offered, out of curiosity.

This is an admirable sort of activity, in that it allows for music making and ensemble participation on the part of those who might otherwise not make music at all (rather like, in some ways, the large choral organizations fielded by communities and universities), and introduces them to repertories of great beauty. The level of expertise is proportional to the requirements for participation, and some such ensembles are looked down upon by "real" music students, or by performers on modern instruments and trained singers.

The amateur status of such ensembles is challenged in those institutions that associate an early-music ensemble with professional training. In some conservatories and music schools there are professional courses in early music, singing, instruments, conducting, and the like. These tend to provide special instruction in instrumental practice—mostly on Baroque instruments—and ensembles of high quality.

This is a tendency of relatively recent vintage; in earlier decades early-music performers prided themselves on discovering personally how early music worked, how their instruments should be played, what the available repertory was. The age of common exploration, however, is giving way to a system of teachers and students, the very system that was partly a cause of the early-music movement at its beginning. Now it is possible simply to be told how to do it, without needing to spend all the time making fruitless experiments; this is in some ways much more efficient, but much less personal, and the knowledge acquired seems perhaps to have less value when simply imparted as doctrine.

The Schola Cantorum Basiliensis has for a long time played an important international role in the study of early music and in the formation of leading performers. Founded by Paul Sacher in 1933, since 1954 it has been part of the City of Basel Music Academy. The school has long been a destination for serious players and singers of early music, particularly in the areas of medieval and

Renaissance music. Among those who have taught there are August Wenzinger (cello and viol), Jordi Savall (viol), Anthony Rooley (lute), Thomas Binkley (lute, medieval music), Andrea von Ramm (voice), Hopkinson Smith (lute), and Edward Tarr (trumpet).

The chief British music schools also have significant early-music courses: the Royal Academy of Music (Historical Performance program), the Royal College of Music (Masters in Historical Performance, early music also integrated into undergraduate programs), and the Royal Northern College of Music (Period Performance, integrated into main program). Specialized programs are found in the Low Countries, the Paris Conservatoire, and many places around the world. In the United States, specialized degree programs are found at twenty-five institutions, including Indiana University, the University of Southern California, Oberlin Conservatory, and the newly established (2009) early-music course at the Juilliard School of Music in New York, and instruction is found in hundreds of U.S. and Canadian universities. Early music has a regular, if secondary, place in the curricula of major music schools.

As early-music degree programs turn out an increasing number of skilled graduates and as professional opportunities for them shrink, many are turning to presenting their own concerts; London, Paris, New York, and Boston have a rich variety of such music. Almost any night of the week one can hear professional-level performers not getting paid to give a concert. Amateurism may be returning in a different and potentially injurious form.

Institutionalization

Since the 1970s, there has been a trend to institutionalize the field of early music. At first it had no name, and it still has none, to the extent that "early music, "historical performance," "performance practice," "authentic instruments," and other such terms are collectively used to describe aspects of this larger phenomenon. But what was once a sort of counterculture, grass-roots participatory phenomenon now has its associations, its institutions, and its journals of record.

A conference in May 1977, held in the Waterloo Room of the Royal Festival Hall in London, was titled "The Future of Early Music in Britain"; it assembled scholars, performers, and others to discuss the phenomenon and to predict the future. A volume of proceedings, edited by J. M. Thomson, was published in 1978, and it makes for interesting reading at a distance of more than thirty years.

A similar, if smaller, conference was held at Oberlin College in 1986/87, and a resulting volume of essays, titled *Authenticity and Early Music* (1988), was edited by Nicholas Kenyon. At the Berkeley Festival in 1990, a panel discussion "The Early Music Debate: Ancients, Moderns, Postmoderns" was published in the *Journal of Musicology* with contributions by Joseph Kerman, Laurence Dreyfus, Joshua Kosman, John Rockwell, Ellen Rosand, Richard Taruskin, and Nicholas McGegan. The proceedings reflect issues of redefinition and a degree of self-doubt. Earlier enthusiasms had turned to serious questions of the feasibility of authenticity, the futility of hoping to re-create anything like real musicianship, and the relativistic questions of whether early music reflects more about our culture than about attitudes of the past.

In 1973 Oxford University Press began publication of the periodical *Early Music*, a handsomely illustrated periodical that included a supplement of newly edited music, and which sought to bring first-rate scholars and performers to the attention of the larger public. The journal continues, at a high scholarly level. *Early Music America* is the quarterly publication of the association Early Music America, continuing its earlier journal *Historical Performance* (1988–94).

A splendidly produced magazine titled *Goldberg* began publication in 1997, producing editions in Spanish, French, and English. It suspended print publication in 2008, continuing as a Web site. *Performance Practice Review,* a peer-reviewed scholarly journal, began publication in 1988 and in 1997 became an electronic journal.

In both Britain and the United States, organizations have tended to begin with associations of players of instruments, recorders (Society of Recorder Players, 1930; American Recorder Society, 1939), viols (Viola da Gamba Society, 1948; Viola da Gamba Society of America, 1962), lutes (Lute Society, ca. 1948; Lute Society of America, 1966). These tend to be associations of players, sometimes with local chapters that facilitate teaching and chamber music, that publish newsletters, directories, and journals.

At a further stage, national associations have grown up with the purpose of furthering the aims of early music and its players. Such associations tend to have a membership of active amateur players, a few professionals, and a number of eager listeners. The National Early Music Association in Britain has published *Early Music Yearbook* since 1993, and a semiannual journal *Early Music Performer*. Early Music America, founded in 1985, supports early-music activities in North America with prizes, workshops, publications, and a variety of other activities.

Early music tomorrow

Early music is getting earlier and earlier; as time moves forward, Bach recedes into the past, and so does Stravinsky (and the Utrecht Festival of 2008 gave an "authentic instruments" performance of *The Rite of Spring*). As is the case with various historical preservation movements, saving space for the materials of the past uses space that might be used for the present and the future. Tearing down a historic house to make way for a new building involves choices.

It need not be so, perhaps, with music. There is plenty of room in the world for music; the competition has to do with commerce, not with art. The amount of money spent on music is enormous, but very little of it is spent on art music; and of the little part of the world dedicated to classical music, that part of it devoted to early music is even tinier. And so the clout of early music is very small indeed.

The power of early music is in the commitment of those dedicated to it by a love of the repertory and by a fascination with the effort of bringing the music of the past alive for audiences of today. That love and fascination will continue to attract more people, and they will continue to develop new ideas and attitudes that will perhaps shock us, and allow them to smile patronizingly at our shallowness and primitiveness.

It is in the eighteenth and nineteenth centuries that opera was the chief entertainment, and the form of art, for much of Western civilization. In the twentieth and twenty-first centuries, despite the great works performed, opera relied largely on the past, and as a spectacle it now has to compete with cinema, rock concerts, sporting events, and other spectacular forms of entertainment.

Many modern opera houses are extending their repertories to include works that once were in the domain of early music: Handel, Cavalli, Monteverdi, Rameau, and others. Early music is moving into the territory of the standard opera repertories: not only Baroque but also Mozart, Beethoven, and other nineteenth-century works are getting the historical treatment.

The rise of Baroque orchestras has led to a sort of cross-pollination with standard symphony orchestras. Baroque orchestras have been able to rise—gradually—to the level of skill and ability of their better-paid and larger competitors, and symphony orchestras have gradually given over to their Baroque counterparts some of the pieces that used to appear much more often on major-symphony programs—Bach passions and the like.

And, perhaps most important, there has been a sort of sharing of insights and talents. Some symphony orchestras have a Baroque orchestra as a subset of their personnel; many symphony players also play a historical instrument, and more than a few orchestras have engaged the talents of conductors who are mostly known for historically informed performance to lead them in repertories and styles that they might not otherwise experience.

In the early part of the twentieth century, most early music was heard in series of early-music concerts organized by museums, institutions, or ensembles. In Boston, for example, concerts of early music were organized in the Houghton Library from 1942 by Erwin Bodky (they were played by members of the Boston Symphony Orchestra); from 1952 the series, renamed as the Cambridge Society for Early Music, presented an annual series of concerts in Sanders Theater at Harvard, consisting primarily of European artists, with a single program performed by local musicians. That series concluded in 1981, mostly as a result of the penetration of early music into the larger concert series of university and presenting organizations. In a sense their mission of bringing early music to a wider audience had succeeded so well that their efforts in that form were no longer necessary. Now the Cambridge Society presents a series of touring concerts in a variety of interesting venues in smaller towns and cities.

The Museum of Fine Arts in Boston sponsored a series of early-music concerts by a group it called the Boston Camerata; from 1968 this group, directed until 2008 by Joel Cohen and more recently by Anne Azéma, became an independent entity, producing concert series and recordings and touring internationally; the Boston Camerata has become a more flexible ensemble, collaborating with a variety of ensembles and artists and often involving cross-cultural music-making.

These are examples of two typical kinds of change going on: the disappearance of early music as a separate entity and its suffusion into mainstream musical life; and the collaboration, crossover, intercultural activities that acknowledge the closeness of early music, in its focus on cultural milieu, to aspects of folk and world music.

The early-music movement grew up in the heyday of the long-playing record, and the magnificent recordings produced in the 1970s and 1980s were a tribute to the companies who supported the efforts, to the artists who produced them, and to the buying public. An early-music label, Das Alte Werk, produced by Telefunken (now Teldec), was begun in 1956 and produced a large quantity of early-music recordings of the first quality. A similarly important early-music series was the Archiv label created in 1947 by Deutsche Grammophon. We should also mention pioneering American labels like Titanic and Dorian. Other European labels include EMI-Reflexe, Harmonia Mundi, and Decca's Oiseau-Lyre. Most, if not all, of these LP recordings are now available on CD from ArkivMusik, Amazon.com, CD Universe, and others.

Another aspect of dissemination is radio, including pioneering programs like David Munrow's Pied Piper on the BBC, or Millennium of Music, Micrologus, and Harmonia, all on National Public Radio in the United States. These latter are programs hosted by an expert, which present music of interest but also topics and information that help the listener become a well-informed early-music aficionado.

Other groups made themselves known through recordings, and the availability of music from the past expanded enormously. It was possible to hear much music on recordings that could not be bought in a published edition. The various Bach cantata projects, the complete works of Byrd, recordings of interesting works of unknown composers, all have the double advantage of bringing to light music that we would not be likely to hear (most of the Bach cantatas had never been recorded before these projects began), and at the same time they bring attention to the recording artists who take the projects on.

The age of the CD prompted the re-release of many of these classic recordings, as well as the production of many more, since the technology of the compact disc was relatively economical, even for small companies or self-publishing ensembles. The modern communication of music electronically is changing rapidly; early-music performers are able to distribute their recordings instantly and worldwide. It remains to be seen how quality will be affected, and how musicians in the future may be able to earn a part of living from their recorded works—but these are not questions limited to early music.

What was at least in part a sort of popular movement has become part of the music industry. Like World Music and Contemporary Music, Early Music as a genre is a niche in the musical world; it has its stars, its schools, its recordings, its students, its established artists, its aspiring ensembles. It is all part of a small professional world.

The amateur aspect of early music, the participatory feeling that this was a music where the distance of amateur and professional was not so great as it has been since the eighteenth century, seems to have diminished considerably since the 1980s. Highly specialized ensembles, a virtuoso level of playing ability, and the fact that training comes not just from self-teaching or from summer workshops but from highly competitive schools of music, have altered the perception of early music for some of its participants.

For those whose enthusiasm was roused by playing the recorder or the viol, by singing madrigals or motets, the chance to learn from a superb teacher, or to hear outstanding soloists and ensembles, was something that added immeasurably to the experience of early music but did not take away the core activity.

At present, there is still a great deal of participatory activity; the local associations still hold workshops and performing events; but the general trend is toward a smaller and older base of participants. Those who fueled the movement with their energy in the 1970s are still doing so, perhaps with as much energy but not in as great a number. And the reinforcements are not appearing.

The increasing canonization of a standard repertory in the nineteenth century has provided us with the necessity, and with the opportunity, to have special concerts of New Music; in the eighteenth century, essentially every concert was a concert of new music. The same trend has brought us Early Music, which is essentially the New Music of an earlier time. New Music and Early Music have much in common: a small, enthusiastic audience; the possibility of hearing a great deal of music one has never heard before; a sense of mission.

However one approaches this music—as part of a continuum of which we are the lucky legatees, or as something newly rediscovered—the music itself continues to fascinate and enrich our world, a world already so full of music that the revival of these earlier repertories is in itself something of a wonder.

Further reading

Works on instruments and performance

Dart, Thurston. *The Interpretation of Music*. London: Hutchinson's University Library, 1954; repr. Harper Colophon, 1988.

Dolmetsch, Arnold. *Interpretation of the Music of the Seventeenth and Eighteenth Centuries*. London: Novello, 1915; repr. Dover, 2005.

Donington, Robert. *The Interpretation of Early Music*. London: Faber and Faber, 1963; rev. ed., W. W. Norton, 1992.

———. *A Performer's Guide to Baroque Music*. London: Faber, 1973; New York: Scribner, 1975.

Hunt, Edgar. *The Recorder and Its Music*. London: L. H. Jenkins, 1962; 2nd ed. 1977, paperback repr. New York: Da Capo, 1982.

Lawson, Colin, and Robin Stowell. *The Historical Performance of Music: An Introduction*. Cambridge: Cambridge University Press, 1999.

Munrow, David. *Instruments of the Middle Ages and Renaissance*. London: Oxford University Press, 1976.

Neumann, Frederick. *Ornamentation in Baroque and Post-Baroque Music with Special Emphasis on J. S. Bach*. Princeton: Princeton University Press, 1973, rev. 1978.

Key treatises on 18th-century music

Bach, Carl Philipp Emanuel. *Essay on the True Art of Playing Keyboard Instruments*. Translation of *Versuch über die wahre Art das Clavier zu spielen* (1753) by William J. Mitchell. New York: Norton, 1949.

Mozart, Leopold. *A Treatise on the Fundamental Principles of Violin Playing*. Translation of *Versuch einer gründlichen Violinschule* (1756) by Editha Knocker. London: Oxford University Press, 1948.

Quantz, Johann Joachim. *On Playing the Flute*. Translation of *Versuch einer Anweisung die Flöte traversiere zu spielen* (1752) by Edward R. Reilly. New York: Schirmer, 1966; exp. ed. 1985; Boston: Northeastern University Press, 2001.

Works on the early-music movement

Butt, John. *Playing with History: The Historical Approach to Musical Performance*. Cambridge: Cambridge University Press, 2002.

Dreyfus, Laurence. "Early Music Defended against Its Devotees: A Theory of Historical Performance in the Twentieth Century." *The Musical Quarterly* 69 (1983): 297–322.

Haskell, Harry. *The Early Music Revival: A History*. New York: Thames and Hudson, 1988.

Haynes, Bruce. *The End of Early Music: A Period Performer's History of Music for the Twenty-First Century*. Oxford: Oxford University Press, 2007.

Kenyon, Nicholas, ed. *Authenticity and Early Music: A Symposium*. Oxford: Oxford University Press, 1988.

Kerman, Joseph, Laurence Dreyfus, Joshua Kosman, John Rockwell, Ellen Rosand, Richard Taruskin, Nicholas McGegan. "The Early Music Debate: Ancients, Moderns, Postmoderns." *Journal of Musicology* 10 (1992): 113–30.

Leech-Wilkinson, Daniel. *The Modern Invention of Medieval Music: Scholarship, Ideology, Performance*. Cambridge: Cambridge University Press, 2002.

Palmer, Larry. *Harpsichord in America: A Twentieth-Century Revival*. Bloomington: Indiana University Press, 1989.

Schott, Howard. "The Harpsichord Revival." *Early Music* 2 (1974): 85–95.

Sherman, Bernard D. *Inside Early Music: Conversations with Performers*. Oxford: Oxford University Press, 1997.

Taruskin, Richard. *Text and Act: Essays on Musical Performance*. New York: Oxford University Press, 1995.

Index

C